I'D GO WITH THE HELMET, RAY

Doonesbury Books by G.B. Trudeau

Still a Few Bugs in the System
The President Is a Lot Smarter Than You Think
But This War Had Such Promise
Call Me When You Find America
Guilty, Guilty, Guilty!
"What Do We Have for the Witnesses, Johnnie?"
Dare to Be Great, Ms. Caucus
Wouldn't a Gremlin Have Been More Sensible?
"Speaking of Inalienable Rights, Amy..."
You're Never Too Old for Nuts and Berries
An Especially Tricky People
As the Kid Goes for Broke
Stalking the Perfect Tan
"Any Grooming Hints for Your Fans, Rollie?"
But the Pension Fund Was Just Sitting There
We're Not Out of the Woods Yet
A Tad Overweight, But Violet Eyes to Die For
And That's My Final Offer!
He's Never Heard of You, Either
In Search of Reagan's Brain
Ask for May, Settle for June
Unfortunately, She Was Also Wired for Sound
The Wreck of the "Rusty Nail"
You Give Great Meeting, Sid
Doonesbury: A Musical Comedy
Check Your Egos at the Door
That's Doctor Sinatra, You Little Bimbo!
Death of a Party Animal
Downtown Doonesbury
Calling Dr. Whoopee
Talkin' About My G-G-Generation
We're Eating More Beets!
Read My Lips, Make My Day, Eat Quiche and Die!
Give Those Nymphs Some Hooters!
You're Smokin' Now, Mr. Butts!

In Large Format

The Doonesbury Chronicles
Doonesbury's Greatest Hits
The People's Doonesbury
Doonesbury Dossier: The Reagan Years
Doonesbury Deluxe: Selected Glances Askance
Recycled Doonesbury: Second Thoughts on a Gilded Age

A DOONESBURY BOOK

by G. B. TRUDEAU

I'D GO WITH THE HELMET, RAY

ANDREWS and McMEEL A UNIVERSAL PRESS SYNDICATE COMPANY KANSAS CITY • NEW YORK

DOONESBURY is distributed internationally by Universal Press Syndicate.

 For information write Andrews and McMeel, a Universal Press Syndicate Company, 4900 Main Street, Kansas City, Missouri 64112.

ISBN: 0-8362-1870-1

Library of Congress Catalog Card Number: 90-85468

"If we get into an armed situation,
he's going to get his ass kicked."

— George Bush, on Saddam Hussein

YOU REALLY GOT ME! YOU REALLY GOT ME! OH, OH, OH!

OKAY, THAT WAS THE KINKS, AND NOW IT'S TIME TO TELL YOU WHO WE ARE! IF YOU CAN'T HANDLE IT, HIT THE VOLUME!

READY? THIS IS NPR, AND YOU'RE TUNED TO... "LITE 'N' EASY ROCK!"

AARRGH!
I KNOW, I KNOW, YOU THOUGHT YOU WERE GETTING DOWN...

... BABY, YOU CAN LIGHT MY FIIIRE!

OKAY, THAT WAS THE DOORS, AND YOU'RE LISTENING TO NPR'S "LITE 'N' EASY ROCK"!

SAY, WANNA KNOW WHO YOU ARE? OUR TARGET AUDIENCE IS LISTED AS "25 TO 54"! CATCH THE TOP END? 54 YEARS OLD! WAY TO GO, GEEZER-HEADS!

WHY DON'T YOU JUST SWITCH STATIONS?
YOU DON'T UNDERSTAND– I LIKE THIS MUSIC!
COMING UP, A SONG RE-LEASED A QUARTER-CENTURY AGO...

HEY, BIG BRO! WHAT'S FOR DINNER?
SAL! YOU LISTEN TO MUSIC–WHAT DO YOU THINK OF THIS?

I CAN'T GET NO... I CAN'T GET NO...

HEY, HEY, HEY! THAT'S WHAT I SAAY! I CAN'T GET NO... SATISFACTION!

WHAT, AM I IN AN ELEVATOR HERE?
I CAN'T STAND IT...
WE'LL HAVE MORE SOOTHING FM-LITE AFTER THIS...

MARK'S RIGHT. I'M COMPLETELY OUT OF TOUCH WITH WHAT'S HAPPENING IN MUSIC NOW!
AW, C'MON, MAN, HOW COULD THAT BE?

I MEAN, YOU'RE HIP TO YOUNG MC, AREN'T YOU? AND MILLI VANILLI? SOUL II SOUL? M BASE? HOW ABOUT PAULA ABDUL? YOU HAVE TO KNOW ABOUT HER, RIGHT?

RIGHT?

I'M MY PARENTS! I'M MY PARENTS!
MIKE, YOU'RE SCARIN' ME HERE, MAN.

SO YOU'RE OUT OF TOUCH WITH POP! BIG DEAL! THE MUSIC DOESN'T ADDRESS ITSELF TO YOU NOW ANYWAY!

BESIDES, IF YOU WANT TO GET INTO THE MUSIC, YOU GOTTA GO LISTEN TO IT! WHEN WAS THE LAST TIME YOU WENT TO A CONCERT?
JUST LAST MONTH! I WENT TO SEE PAUL McCARTNEY!

PAUL McCARTNEY? =COUGH!..=
YEAH!

I FORGET. WAS HE THE SMART MOPHEAD?
THE CUTE ONE! AND DON'T YOU PATRONIZE ME!

YOU KNOW, BIG BRO, POP MUSIC HAS ALWAYS BEEN EXCLUSIONARY! IT'S AIMED AT THE YOUNG AND THE RESTLESS! YOU'RE NOT SUPPOSED TO GET IT!

WELL, I MIGHT BE ABLE TO GET IT IF THEY'D PUT THE MELODY BACK IN!
HEY, THAT'S WHAT BIG BAND SAID ABOUT ROCK! AND WHAT ROCK SAID ABOUT DISCO!

EACH GENERATION HAS MOVED POP FORWARD RHYTHMICALLY. RAP IS MOSTLY PERCUSSION—USUALLY NO MELODY AT ALL! THE MUSIC IS FOR MOVIN' TO NOW, AND YOUR AGE DOESN'T DANCE ANYMORE!

HEY, I DO! I'VE JUST GOT A BAD BACK!
HANG ON, SLOOPY, SLOOPY, HANG ON!
ROCK ON, BABE. LATER.

THE DONALD COULD BARELY CONTAIN HIM-SELF.
THIS IS BIG!

I'D LIKE TO CONFIRM THE RUMORS THAT MARCIE WILL BE ATTENDING THE TRUMP TAJ OPENING! AND SHE'S GOING TO KNOCK YOUR SOCKS OFF! BELIEVE ME, THIS KID HAS A BIG, I MEAN BIG, FUTURE!

BY THE END OF THE EVENING, MARILYN MAPLES WILL BE THE HOTTEST NAME IN THE WORLD! THE HOTTEST! I GUARANTEE IT!

MEANWHILE. BACK AT THE SAFE HOUSE...
WHAT WILL I WEAR?
GB Trudeau

AND ON APRIL 5, EXCLUSIVELY AT THE TRUMP TAJ, I WILL BE UNVEILING THE TRUMP ESCORT!

MARLIE MAPLES IS ABOUT TO BECOME A HOUSEHOLD NAME! I GUARANTEE IT! IT'S EVEN RU-MORED THAT I'VE GOT A MIL-LION DOLLAR BET ON IT!

MARY WILL BE SETTING A NEW STANDARD FOR THE INDUSTRY! SHE'S THE HOTTEST, SLEEKEST, BEST-BUILT, MOST GLAMOROUS MODEL IN THE WORLD!

SHE SOUNDS LIKE A NEW CAR.
THERE'S THAT KIND OF EXCITE-MENT, YES.
GB Trudeau

ANY MORE QUESTIONS? NOTHING SENSATIONAL-ISTIC, PLEASE.

DONNIE, YOU'VE HAD QUITE A BUSY TWO YEARS, WHAT WITH THE PLAZA, THE SHUTTLE, THE BOAT, THE BIKE RACE, ETC.

WHAT A LOT OF PEOPLE WOULD LIKE TO KNOW IS HOW'D YOU FIND THE TIME TO BECOME SUCH "GOOD FRIENDS" WITH MS. MAPLES?

WHATEVER HAPPENS, I'LL... I'LL NEVER FORGET OUR SEC-ONDS TOGETHER!
©B Trudeau

HEY, MARLA MAPLES! YOU'VE JUST BEEN INVITED TO A CASINO OPENING BY THE MOST FAMOUS ADULTERER ON THE PLANET!
I KNOW! I'M GOING AS A FAVOR!

WHAT WILL YOU WEAR? WHO WILL DO YOUR HAIR? HOW WILL YOU KEEP IT FROM GETTING MESSED UP BY THE HELICOPTER PROP WASH?

UM...

AND HOW WILL YOU PORTRAY YOURSELF TO THE PRESS—AS VICTIMIZED BIMBO OR GOLD-DIGGING MISTRESS?

HMM...
DECISIONS, DECISIONS!

MARLO? DONALD HERE.
OH, DONNIE, I...

NO TIME TO CHAT. JUST WANTED TO BRING YOU UP TO SPEED ON THE TAJ OPENING!

I'VE TAKEN CARE OF EVERYTHING, JEWELRY, DRESS, HAIR, THE WORKS! I'M ALSO FLYING IN A TRAINER FOR YOU—I WANT YOU TO EXERCISE AND DIET RIGHT UP TO OPENING NIGHT! GOT IT?

HOW ABOUT SURGERY? SHOULD I HAVE SURGERY?
THERE'S NO TIME! GOTTA RUN, BABE!
CLIK!
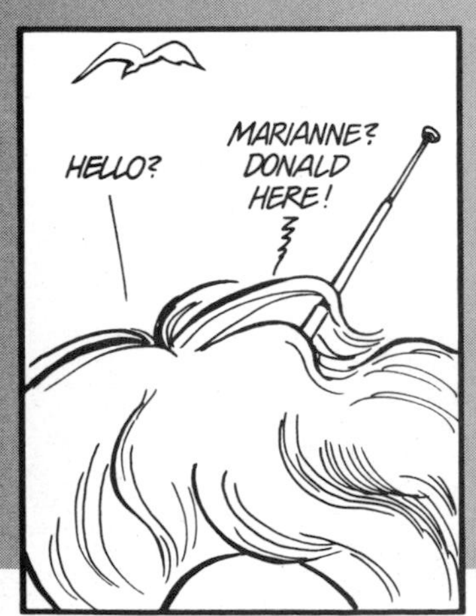
HELLO?
MARIANNE? DONALD HERE!

LISTEN, KID, I KNOW ALL OF THIS HAS BEEN ROUGH ON YOU, SO I JUST WANTED TO CALL AND LET YOU KNOW HOW MUCH I STILL CARE FOR YOU!

DONNIE?... WHAT'S WRONG WITH YOUR VOICE?
UH... NOTHING...

YOU'RE NOT DON! WHO IS THIS?
UM... HIS ASSISTANT. MR. TRUMP'S TIED UP TODAY.

HEROES.
MARLA? WE **LOVE** HER HERE IN DALTON!
SHE'S MY HERO! I'M TRYING TO GET MY HAIR TO DO WHAT HERS DOES!

HEY, I USED TO DATE HER IN HIGH SCHOOL, AND WHAT CAN I TELL YOU—THE CHICK'S **GOT** IT! I THINK SHE'S GONNA BE BIGGER THAN DONNA RICE!
DEERE

I THINK SHE'S GREAT! A REAL GEORGIA PEACH! MARLA, WE LOVE YA, HONEY!
A OK
PRICED TO MOVE!
$300.MO

EVERYONE I KNOW REALLY ADMIRES HER A LOT!
ADMIRES HER? FOR HAVING AN AFFAIR WITH A MARRIED MILLIONAIRE?

BILLIONAIRE!
SHE'S THE PRIDE OF DALTON! THERE'S EVEN TALK OF RE-NAMING THE MALL AFTER HER!

MEANWHILE, IN QUEENS...
JOHN GOTTI? SORT OF A PERSONAL HERO.
SUCH A NICE MAN! WE ALL THINK THE WORLD OF HIM!
GBTrudeau

MAN... TRUMP JUST DOESN'T LET UP, DOES HE?
SPORTS
New York DAILY NEW
Marla to Ivana
TRUMP

YOU KNOW WHO I FEEL THE MOST SORRY FOR HERE?
I HOPE IT'S NOT MISS MAPO. SHE REALLY BOUGHT INTO THE WHOLE THING!

NO, I FEEL SORRY FOR THE PRESS. THOSE GUYS SHOULD BE DRAWING HARDSHIP PAY!

AND I'LL BE SLEEPING WITH MAJOR STARS! MAJOR! I HAVE OFFERS!
CAN WE GO NOW?

AND NOW A SPECIAL TREAT FOR ALL YOU "CLASSIC" ROCKERS! SITTING NEXT TO ME IS OUR OLD FRIEND, THE PRINCE OF LITENESS HIMSELF – MR. JAMES THUDPUCKER!

THANKS, MARK. TODAY I'D LIKE TO SHARE WITH YOUR LISTENERS SOME OF MY CONCERNS ABOUT OZONE DEPLETION, DEFORESTATION, GLOBAL WARMING – THE WHOLE GAMUT OF TRANSBOUNDARY ENVIRONMENTAL THREATS!

YOU WOULD?
YES. IS THAT A PROBLEM?

UH... WE'RE IN A BIT OF A RATINGS SLUMP, JIM. COULD YOU WORK THE TRUMPS IN?
YOU'VE CHANGED, MARK.

MARK, THE FIRST SONG ON MY NEW ALBUM IS ABOUT DEFORESTATION. IT'S BEING RELEASED ON APRIL 22, TO OBSERVE EARTH DAY!

SOUNDS INTENSE. LET'S CUE IT UP.
IT'S CALLED "THE UNKINDEST CUT."

GET DOWN, HOMES, MY NAME IS JIMMY T! WE CAN ROCK THE HOUSE, OR WE CAN SAVE A TREE! HUNH!

THAT'S A DIFFERENT SOUND FOR YOU, ISN'T IT, JIM?
KIND OF. IT'S NOT SO FOLKY.
HUNH! YO! OW!

I GUESS IF MY MUSIC SOUNDS A LITTLE DIFFERENT NOW, MARK, IT'S BECAUSE **I'M** DIFFERENT. I'M NO LONGER A KID WRITING FOR AND ABOUT OTHER KIDS.

I'VE TALKED TO MICK AND ROD ABOUT THIS, AND THEY BOTH AGREE OUR MUSIC IS NEVER AGAIN GOING TO MEAN TO OUR LISTENERS WHAT IT DID WHEN WE WERE ALL YOUNG.

I MEAN, WHAT'S THE "CLASSIC ROCK" AUDIENCE — 25 TO 54? 54? **THINK** OF THAT! WE'RE TALKING ABOUT AN **ENTIRELY** DIFFERENT SET OF CONCERNS NOW!

LIKE WHAT?
WELL, LIKE, MY FANS ARE BEGINNING TO HAVE THEIR FIRST HEART ATTACKS. I HAVE TO **SPEAK** TO THAT!

YOU SEE, MARK, ROCK 'N' ROLL WAS ORIGINALLY ABOUT GIVING VOICE TO RAW, UNPROCESSED EMOTIONS — THE FIRESTORMS OF ADOLESCENCE!

I ACCEPT THAT. I DON'T EVEN **TRY** TO TAP INTO IT ANYMORE. IT'S UNDIGNIFIED. INSTEAD, I'M SPEAKING TO THE EVOLVING CONCERNS OF THE MATURE LISTENER.

INDEED YOU ARE, JAMES. AND IN THAT VEIN, WHY DON'T WE CLOSE WITH YOUR LATEST, "ME LOSIN' YOU"! LIKE TO SAY ANYTHING ABOUT IT?

SURE. IT'S A LITTLE REGGAE NUMBER ABOUT GUM DISEASE.
AND IT'S A TOE-TAPPER, FOLKS! ENJOY!
SIGH...

BY MOST ACCOUNTS, PEDRO WAS AN EXQUISITELY CARVED DOLL, FAIRLY GLISTENING IN HIS MULTI-COLORED COATS OF LACQUER.

LOVINGLY CRAFTED BY AN ANDEAN CAMPESINO, HE WAS FIRST PLACED IN A LOCAL SOUVENIR SHOP IN 1973.

THERE HE LANGUISHED, UNSOLD, FOR 17 YEARS. NOBODY, IT SEEMED, WANTED AN ANATOMICALLY EXPLICIT GAG DOLL.
GBTrudeau

THEN, ONE DAY, PEDRO'S LUCK CHANGED...
HA, HA! HONEY! LOOK AT THIS!
SPROING!

ON A SCHEDULED SHOP-OP IN THE CHILEAN HIGHLANDS, DAN QUAYLE DISCOVERS PEDRO, AN ANATOMICALLY EXPLICIT GAG DOLL.
HA, HA! NOW, THAT'S CLEVER!
THWIP! THWIP!

AS A STUNNED PRESS CORPS LOOKS ON, AMERICA'S GOOD-WILL AMBASSADOR STUDIES THE OBSCENE CURIO.

THE VICE PRESIDENT, ALREADY SUFFERING FROM A MAJOR IMAGE PROBLEM, WEIGHS THE RISKS AND REACHES A QUICK DECISION.

I'LL TAKE IT!
AN EXCELLENT SELECTION, SEÑOR!
GBTrudeau

UP AND DOWN THE REMOTE CHILEAN VALLEY...

THE WORD WAS SPREAD!
CEZA
Coca Cola

AFTER 17 YEARS...

PEDRO, THE ANATOMICALLY EXPLICIT DOLL, HAD BEEN SOLD!
SPROING!
HA, HA! IS THAT GREAT?
GBTrudeau

AT HIS BOSS'S BIDDING, A SECRET SERVICE AGENT PRESSED A FEW DOLLARS INTO THE OLD SHOPKEEPER'S HAND...

...AND PEDRO, THE ANATOMICALLY EXPLICIT GAG DOLL WAS QUICKLY SPIRITED OUT OF TOWN...

...AND ONTO THE AWAITING AIR FORCE TWO...
UNITED STATES OF AM

...WHERE IT CONTINUED TO EMBARRASS EVERYONE.
DANNY! GET THAT OUT OF HERE!
HEE, HEE! WHAT A RIOT!
THWAT!
GB Trudeau

IT WAS AN ASTONISHING TURN OF EVENTS FOR PEDRO, THE ANATOMICALLY EXPLICIT GAG DOLL.

FOR 17 LONG YEARS, HE HAD SAT, IGNORED, ON A DUSTY SHELF IN A CHILEAN SOUVENIR STALL.

BUT NOW, AS AIR FORCE TWO TOUCHED DOWN ON U.S. SOIL, IT SEEMED THE LITTLE DOLL'S STORY WAS ABOUT TO END HAPPILY.

IN FACT, IT WAS JUST BEGINNING.
FOR ME? WHAT IS IT?
HEE, HEE! STAND BACK, SIR!
GB Trudeau

GEORGE?
COME IN, BAR. I'LL BE THROUGH IN A MINUTE...

... I'M JUST GOING OVER THE REPORTS ON DANNY'S TRIP TO SOUTH AMERICA.

HOW'D HE DO?
WELL, THERE WERE A FEW BUMPS. BUT NOTHING TOO SERIOUS.
GB Trudeau

GREAT! DID HE BRING YOU THIS CUTE LITTLE...
NO! DON'T...
SPROING!

THE WHITE HOUSE CABINET ROOM. THE INNER SANCTUM OF THE UPPER REACHES, CLOSED TO ALL— UNTIL **NOW!** LET'S TAKE A LIVE PEEK...

GOOD MORNING, MR. PRESIDENT!
ROLAND! YOU LOOK WELL!
SO DO YOU, SIR! MAY WE COME IN?
PLEASE DO! I WAS JUST MAKING SOME TOUGH CALLS!

WELCOME TO CONSENSUS CITY! I'M ROLAND HEDLEY, AND THIS IS "30 MINUTES IN THE LIFE OF THE WHITE HOUSE, LIVE."
WE WERE JUST GOING OVER TODAY'S AGENDA! WHAT'S NEXT, BOYS?

AN ARRAY OF CRITICAL POLICY DECISIONS THAT WILL AFFECT THIS COUNTRY WELL INTO THE NEXT CENTURY, MR. PRESIDENT!
GREAT! LET ME **AT** 'EM!

I KNOW WE'RE GOING TO TAKE SOME HEAT ON SOME OF THESE. BUT, HEY, THAT'S WHAT I'M PAID FOR! BEING PRESIDENT ISN'T A **POPULARITY CONTEST!**

GEORGE BUSH. CAUGHT IN THE ACT OF BEING HIMSELF.
WHOA! THE CAMERA'S STILL HERE?
YOU SHOULDN'T LET YOUR GUARD DOWN LIKE THAT, SIR.
GBTrudeau

COUNTING THE HOMELESS.
FOUND ONE, EDDIE! HELLO?... EXCUSE ME?
U.S. CENSUS BUREAU

YES?... GOOD GRAVY! IT'S THE CENSUS BOYS!
YES, MA'AM. SORRY TO DISTURB YOU SO LATE AT NIGHT.

WHAT'S GOING ON? WHAT'S ALL THIS TALK ABOUT GRAVY?
LOVELY NEWS, EL! IT'S TIME TO STAND UP AND BE COUNTED!
CENSUS BUREAU, SIR.

OKAY, OKAY! ONE, TWO, YOU COUNTED US! NOW AM-SCRAY!
YOU DON'T UNDERSTAND. WE'RE FROM THE GOVERNMENT. THERE ARE FORMS.
ZIP!

THINK I COULD GET YOU TO FILL OUT THIS CENSUS FORM, MA'AM?
COULD YOU? I'VE BEEN WAITING TEN YEARS FOR THIS, DUCKS...

...UH... BUT I CAN'T DO IT RIGHT NOW. I DON'T WANT TO MISS THE NEW WILDLIFE SPECIAL AT 10:00!

WHAT, YOU'VE GOT A TV IN THERE?
NO, MY HUSBAND ELMONT.

THE MALE YAK APPROACHES HIS MATE CAUTIOUSLY...
OOPS, ALREADY STARTED!

WELL, DUCKS, I FILLED THIS OUT THE BEST I COULD.
ME, TOO!
U.S. CENSUS BUREAU

WHAT?
I THINK I ACED IT, TOO! THE QUESTIONS WERE RIDICULOUSLY EASY!

ELMONT, HOW COULD YOU FILL OUT THAT FORM?
EASY! I CRAMMED ALL NIGHT!

BUT ELMONT— YOU'RE ILLITERATE.
WRONG! I KNEW BOTH MY PARENTS! COULDN'T BE NICER PEOPLE!

ELMONT, I CAN'T QUITE MAKE OUT ALL YOUR ANSWERS HERE, SO LET'S GO OVER THEM, OKAY? "HOW IS PERSON 2 RELATED TO PERSON 1?"

ELMONT AND I ARE MARRIED.
WE MOST CERTAINLY ARE **NOT!**

YES, WE ARE, BABE.
WE ARE **NOT!**
YES, WE ARE.
WE ARE **NOT!**
WE ARE, HUN.
NO WAY, JOSÉ!

OKAY, YOU WIN, DUCKS. WE'RE MARRIED.
HAPPILY SO! NINE YEARS! **TWENTY**, MAYBE!
YOU'RE A LUCKY MAN, PERSON 1.

YOU GOT QUITE A JOB COUNTING THE HOMELESS, DUCKS! IS ANYONE HELPING YOU?
U.S. CENSUS

YOU MIGHT SAY THAT. THERE ARE 15,000 CENSUS TAKERS NATIONWIDE, MANY OF THEM HOMELESS THEMSELVES.
YOU GOT STREET FOLKS COUNTING **THEMSELVES?**

HAVE TO. THEY'RE THE ONLY ONES WHO REALLY KNOW WHERE ALL THE SPECIAL HOMELESS HIDEOUTS ARE.

YO, MANNY! HOW MANY KIDS YOU GOT?
SURPRISE ME.

I GOTTA TELL YA, DUCKS, I'M A LITTLE SKEPTICAL YOU CAN FIND ALL OF US IN ONE NIGHT!
WE ARE, TOO, ALICE...

WE **KNOW** WE'LL MISS A LOT OF PEOPLE. THE PURPOSE OF THE CENSUS IS TO ESTABLISH A BASELINE, A FRAMEWORK FOR DISCUSSING THE HOMELESS...
WHAT ABOUT THE **HOPELESS?**
U.S. CENSUS

WHAT ABOUT THE **HELPLESS?** WHAT ABOUT THE **ROOTLESS?** WHAT ABOUT THE **TOOTHLESS?** WHAT ABOUT THE **YOUNG** AND THE **RESTLESS?**

WE'RE COUNTING THEM, TOO, ELMONT.
WHY? WHAT MAKES **THEM** SO SPECIAL? HAVE THEY DONE **LETTERMAN?**
EARTH TO ELMONT. WHAT IS YOUR POSITION?

RISE AND SHINE, EARTHLINGS! IT'S A BRAND-NEW DAY IN THE GREENHOUSE! 5:45 A.M., TO BE PRECISE!

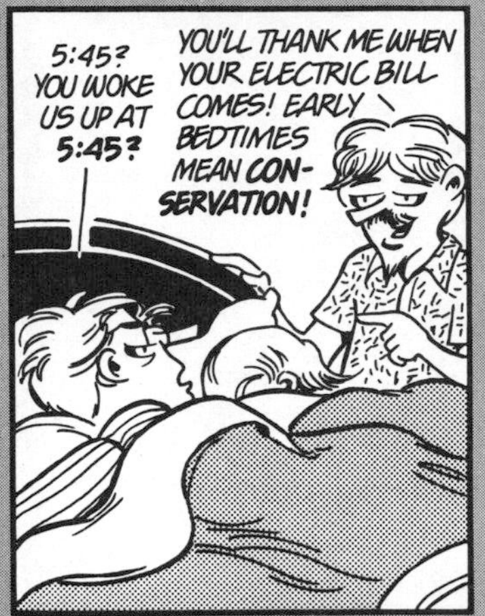
5:45? YOU WOKE US UP AT 5:45?
YOU'LL THANK ME WHEN YOUR ELECTRIC BILL COMES! EARLY BEDTIMES MEAN CONSERVATION!

TIME TO DO OUR PART! THREE-MINUTE SHOWERS! SEPARATED GARBAGE! BRICKS IN THE TOILET! YES, IT'S TIME TO GET WITH THE PROGRAM-IT'S EARTH MONTH!

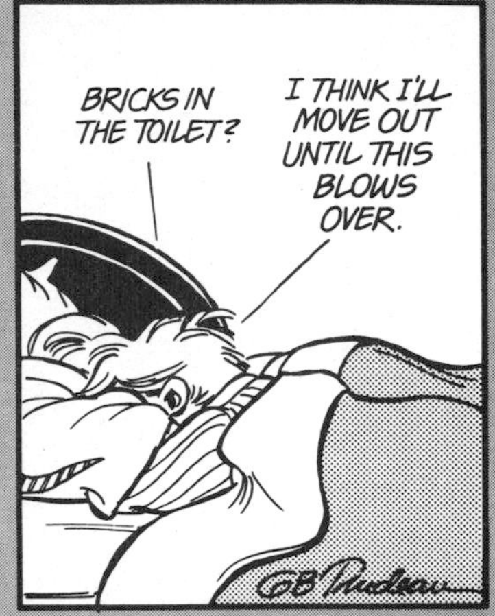
BRICKS IN THE TOILET?
I THINK I'LL MOVE OUT UNTIL THIS BLOWS OVER.

MORNING, FELLOW SPACESHIP EARTHMATE!
I CAN'T BELIEVE YOU WOKE US ALL UP AT DAWN!

EARLY TO RISE, EARLY TO BED! AND THAT MEANS ENERGY CONSERVATION! ESPECIALLY WITH THESE NEW SCREW-IN FLUORESCENTS!

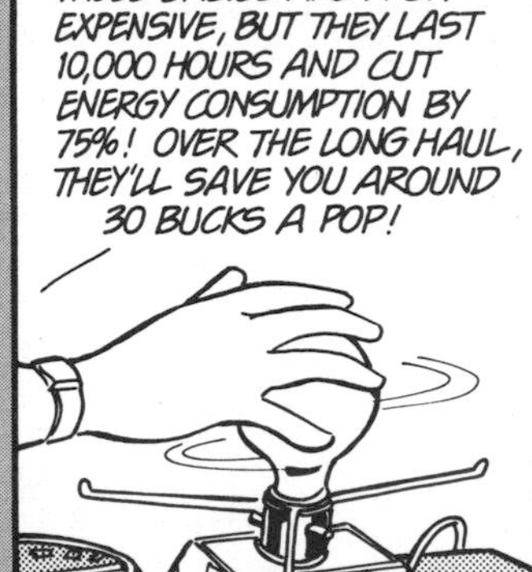
THESE BABIES ARE A BIT EXPENSIVE, BUT THEY LAST 10,000 HOURS AND CUT ENERGY CONSUMPTION BY 75%! OVER THE LONG HAUL, THEY'LL SAVE YOU AROUND 30 BUCKS A POP!

OH, BY THE WAY, I CHANGED THE SHOWER HEAD, TOO!
PWIT!

GO EASY ON THE HOT WATER, OKAY, MIKE?
DO I HAVE A CHOICE?
PWIT!
PLIP!
PLOP!

I INSTALLED THAT LOW-FLOW SHOWER HEAD MYSELF! GREAT, HUH?
YEAH, GREAT.
FOOSH!

BETWEEN THE THREE OF US, WE SHOULD SAVE 15,000 GALLONS A YEAR!
LISTEN, ZONK...
PLOP
PLOP

I ALSO PUT A TIMER ON THE LIGHT.
CLIK!
ZIP!
AIEE!

HI, IS THIS FOOD-MART? YEAH, DO YOUR DELIVERY GUYS USE BIKES OR VANS? BIKES? GREAT! I'D LIKE TO ORDER SOME GROCERIES!
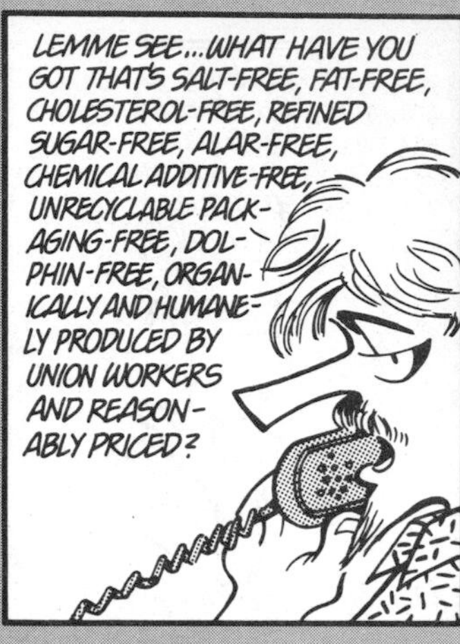
LEMME SEE... WHAT HAVE YOU GOT THAT'S SALT-FREE, FAT-FREE, CHOLESTEROL-FREE, REFINED SUGAR-FREE, ALAR-FREE, CHEMICAL ADDITIVE-FREE, UNRECYCLABLE PACKAGING-FREE, DOLPHIN-FREE, ORGANICALLY AND HUMANELY PRODUCED BY UNION WORKERS AND REASONABLY PRICED?

OKAY... GOOD. I'LL TAKE A DOZEN. THE NAME'S DOONESBURY. 141 AVENUE B. APARTMENT 4-B. OKAY? THANKS.
©B Trudeau

SO WHAT'S FOR DINNER?
POT HOLDERS.

DON'T FORGET TO TAKE YOUR MUG TO WORK, MIKE. DISPOSABLE COFFEE CUPS ARE A NO-NO!
SO'S FORGETTING TO GET ALEX TO THE DENTIST ON TIME. YOU'VE GOT TEN MINUTES.

NO PROBLEM! IT'S ONLY A BLOCK TO... OH, NO!
WHAT?

I CAN'T DO IT, MIKE! YOU'LL HAVE TO TAKE ALEX YOURSELF!
ZIP!
WHAT IS IT? WHAT'S WRONG?

I FORGOT TO PUT OUT THE DRYER LINT FOR NEST-BUILDING BIRDS!
EXCUSE ME? WILL THIS BE OVER SOON?
©B Trudeau

UH... ZONKER? DID YOU LEAVE THE LID OFF THE DIAPER PAIL?
NOPE! I TOOK ALEX OFF PAMPERS!
SNIFF! SNIFF!

YOU WHAT?
I HAD TO, MIKE. DISPOSABLES AREN'T RECYCLED. AND CLOTH'S NO BETTER! THE ENERGY USED TO MAKE AND LAUNDER CLOTH DIAPERS EXCEEDS THAT OF DISPOSABLES! PLUS YOU GET DELIVERY TRUCK EXHAUST!

I SEE. SO WHAT'S SHE WEARING?
NOTHING.
©B Trudeau

NOTHING?
HOLD THE FORT, WILLYA? I GOTTA TAKE YOUR BEDSPREAD DOWN TO THE CLEANERS.

DON'T YOU SEE, MIKE? WE GOTTA STOP FOULING OUR HABITAT! SURE, WE CALL OURSELVES ENVIRONMENTALISTS, BUT WHAT HAVE YOU DONE LATELY TO SAVE THE PLANET?

FOR INSTANCE, HAVE YOU (CHECK ONE OR MORE): 1. □ SEPARATED YOUR REUSABLES FROM YOUR COMPOSTABLES; 2. □ BOYCOTTED PVC'S; 3. □ INVESTED IN DURABLES; 4. □ SENSITIZED A LOCAL OFFICIAL?
UM...

FOR INSTANCE, HAVE YOU (CHECK ONE OR MORE): 1. ☑ SEPARATED YOUR REUSABLES FROM YOUR COMPOSTABLES; 2. □ BOYCOTTED PVC'S; 3. □ INVESTED IN DURABLES 4. □ SENSITIZED A LOCAL ICIAL?
LET'S SEE...
HE'S GETTING TO ME...

MIKE?... WHAT TIME IS IT?
5:30. I DECIDED ZONKER HAS A POINT. MAYBE WE SHOULD BE GETTING UP EARLIER TO CONSERVE ENERGY.

MIKE, JUST BECAUSE ZONKER'S LOST HIS MIND DOESN'T MEAN YOU HAVE TO LOSE YOURS! GIVE YOURSELF A BREAK, WILLYA? YOU HAVE THE MOST OVERWROUGHT CONSCIENCE IN AMERICA!

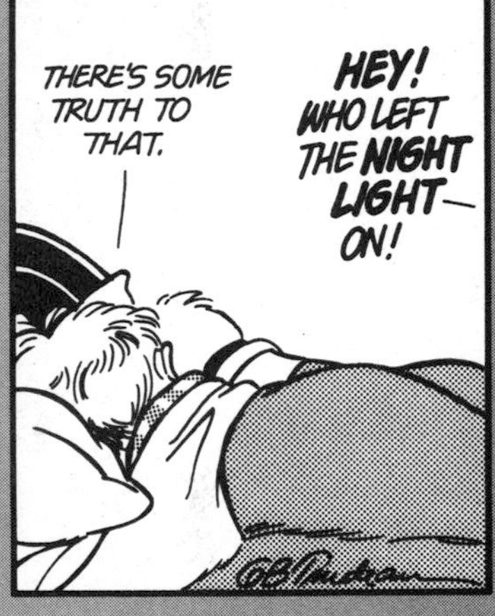
THERE'S SOME TRUTH TO THAT.
HEY! WHO LEFT THE NIGHT LIGHT— ON!

HEY, MARCIA? I NEED TO GET RID OF THIS FOIL GUM WRAPPER...

DO YOU THINK I SHOULD PUT IT WITH THE RECYCLABLE ALUMINUMS OR THE REUSABLE PAPER? ACTUALLY, IT'S NOT REALLY ALUMINUM, IS IT?

BUT THEN, IT'S NOT PAPER, EITHER. MAYBE I SHOULD PUT IT IN THE TOXIN BIN, TO BE SAFE. BUT THEN, THAT JUST ADDS TO THE SOLID-WASTE DISPOSAL PROBLEM, DOESN'T IT?

NEVER MIND, I'LL JUST EAT IT... NO...
CELEBRATING EARTH DAY A LITTLE EARLY, ARE WE?

ZONK? MIKE. I'M HAVING LUNCH OUT TODAY. ANY GUIDELINES?
YEAH, STAY AWAY FROM THE SHELLFISH. IT'S PROBABLY FROM THE SOUND, WHICH IS BADLY POLLUTED.

ALSO, NO TUNA STEAK UNTIL THEY STOP KILLING DOLPHINS IN THE TUNA NETS. AND FORGET MEAT AND DAIRY PRODUCTS—THE FARMS ARE INHUMANELY RUN AND THE STUFF'S BAD FOR YOU ANYWAY...

ALSO, IF YOU USE THE SALAD BAR, MAKE SURE THE VEGETABLES HAVE BEEN RINSED OF RADIOACTIVE DUST AND PESTICIDES!
UH... OKAY. THANKS.

PERRIER OKAY?
I'LL HAVE THE WATER.
MENU
GB Trudeau

I CAN'T BELIEVE MYSELF... I PASS UP SALADS, ONLY TO BUY A HOT DOG!
HOT

THE **LOOKS** I'M GETTING! EVERYONE KNOWS WHAT'S **IN** ONE OF THESE! I CAN FEEL THEIR HOT DISAPPROVAL!

HOPE YOU ENJOY YOUR **MEAT!**
THERE GOES ANOTHER **RAIN FOREST!**
LOOK! HE'S WEARING **LEATHER SHOES,** TOO!
ASSASSIN!
POLLUTER!
MUNCH! MUNCH!

MAYBE IF I STAND ABSOLUTELY STILL...
LOOK AT HIM STANDING THERE **SPEWING OUT** CO_2!
GB Trudeau

OKAY, MIKE, SEE YOU TONIGHT. YOU'RE BIKING IT, RIGHT?
NO, I'M NOT BIKING IT! I'M **TIRED!** LISTEN, Z, YOU GOTTA CUT ME SOME SLACK...

I CAN'T SPEND ALL DAY SUBJECTING MY EVERY ACTION TO ECO-ANALYSIS! IT'S DRIVING ME NUTS!

IF I CONSIDER THE IMPACT OF EVERYTHING I DO, I'LL NEVER GET OUT OF BED! I'LL JUST LIE THERE ALL DAY, LIGHTS OFF, HEAT OFF, MUNCHING ORGANICALLY GROWN CELERY!

THAT'S A PROBLEM?
GB Trudeau

GOOD MORNING. AS SOME OF YOU MAY KNOW, I'VE BEEN TAKING A LOT OF HEAT FROM THE ENVIRONMENTAL CROWD LATELY...
abc

NOT THAT I CAN'T TAKE THE HEAT FROM THESE EXTREMIST GUYS. I CAN. BUT AS THE ENVIRONMENT PRESIDENT, I SHOULDN'T **HAVE** TO!
8 NEWS

THE THING OF IT IS, THESE ENVIRONMENTAL PROBLEMS ARE LOCAL! THE **STATES** AREN'T DOING THE JOB THEY SHOULD BE, AND AS THE ENVIRONMENT PRESIDENT, I'VE TOLD THEM SO!

SURE, CLEANING UP THE ENVIRONMENT COSTS MONEY, BUT MONEY MEANS TOUGH CHOICES AND/OR TAXES, AND THAT GOES AGAINST THE VERY GRAIN OF MY APPROVAL RATINGS!

WHAT TO DO? WELL, THIS ADMINISTRATION HAS ALWAYS TAKEN ITS INSPIRATION FROM A WORD FOUND IN NATURE ITSELF...

COAST.
©B Trudeau

IN PANAMA, THE BLOOM IS OFF THE INVASION...
WHAT DID BUSH BRING US BUT MORE POVERTY AND DEATH?

THOUSANDS OF OUR HOMES WERE DESTROYED, BUT STILL WE SEE NO AID! WE MUST TAKE OUR COUNTRY BACK! WE MUST SEND THE PROCONSUL PACKING!

YANQUI GO HOME!
YANQUI GO HOME!

NOT MUCH OF A LIKENESS.
CLOSE ENOUGH, SIR.
©B Trudeau

ANTI-U.S. RIOTS! AFTER ALL I'VE DONE FOR THIS RAT-HOLE OF A COUNTRY!
I CAN IMAGINE HOW THAT MIGHT BE DEMORALIZING, SIR...

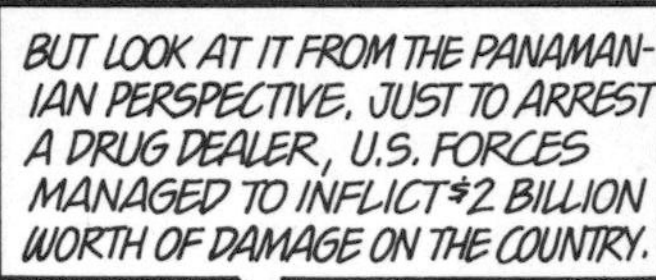
BUT LOOK AT IT FROM THE PANAMANIAN PERSPECTIVE. JUST TO ARREST A DRUG DEALER, U.S. FORCES MANAGED TO INFLICT $2 BILLION WORTH OF DAMAGE ON THE COUNTRY.

IN THE ABSENCE OF NO AID WHATSOEVER, THOUSANDS ARE STILL HOMELESS. SOME ARE EVEN LIVING UNDER CLUSTERS OF PARACHUTES ABANDONED BY THE VERY SOLDIERS WHOSE ARRIVAL LEFT THEM HOMELESS!

CHEAP, THIRD WORLD IRONY! I WON'T STAND FOR IT!
THEY CALL IT "SCREAMING EAGLE ESTATES."
ZIP!
©B Trudeau

I DON'T BELIEVE IT! YOU WERE RIGHT, HONEY! THERE ARE PEOPLE LIVING UNDER PARACHUTES!
YES, SIR. FOR FOUR MONTHS NOW.

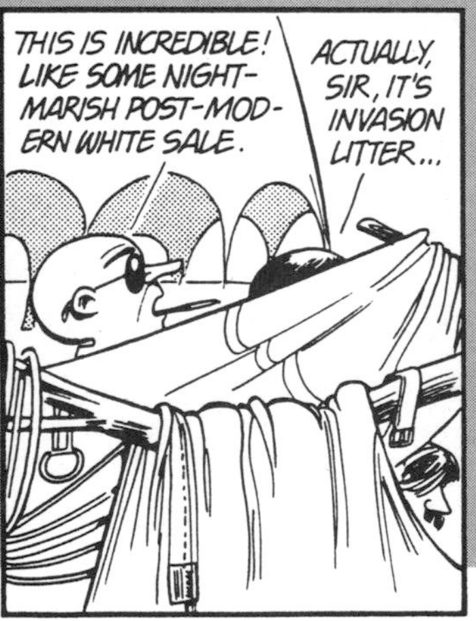
THIS IS INCREDIBLE! LIKE SOME NIGHTMARISH POST-MODERN WHITE SALE.
ACTUALLY, SIR, IT'S INVASION LITTER...

...BUT WITHOUT IT, THESE PEOPLE WOULD HAVE NO SHELTER AT ALL! IT MEANS A LOT YOUR COMING DOWN HERE, SIR. IT SHOWS YOU CARE!
©B Trudeau

YEAH, BUT I DON'T. THIS WOULD MAKE A HELLUVA THEME PARK, WOULDN'T IT?
YOU CAN'T FOOL ME, SIR.

SEÑORA! I'M TOLD YOU AND OTHERS MAKE YOUR HOMES HERE AMONG THE PARACHUTES! HOW REMARKABLE!

THERE'S SOMETHING VISIONARY HERE! PARACHUTE DOMICILES! COOL, DRY, STRONG, ILLUMINATED BY SOFT, FILTERED LIGHT! THIS IS THE FUTURE! IT WORKS!

I SEE A CITY, SEÑORA! A SILK CITY! 1,000 SHIMMERING UNITS STRUNG ACROSS THE HILLS! WHAT DO YOU SAY TO THAT?

LAST NIGHT, WE BURNED YOU IN EFFIGY.
OKAY, 2,000! BUT ANY MORE AND YOU'LL ATTRACT RODENTS.
GB Trudeau

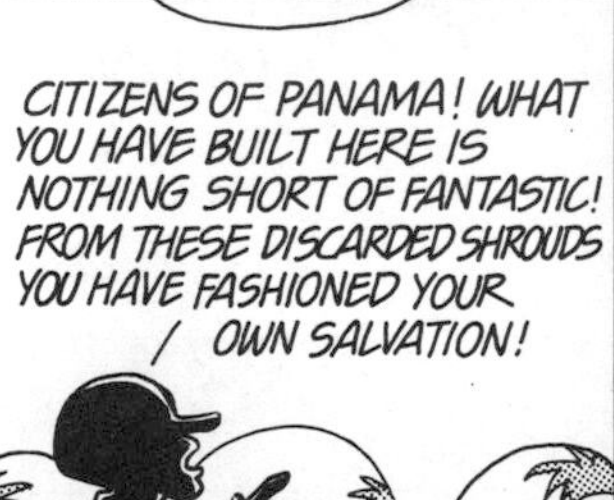
CITIZENS OF PANAMA! WHAT YOU HAVE BUILT HERE IS NOTHING SHORT OF FANTASTIC! FROM THESE DISCARDED SHROUDS YOU HAVE FASHIONED YOUR OWN SALVATION!

IT IS NOW MY PRIVILEGE TO DEDICATE "SCREAMING EAGLE ESTATES" TO THE MEMORY OF YOUR FOUNDING FATHERS — THE 82ND AIRBORNE! CHEERS!

C'MON, HONEY, LET'S GET TO OUR NEXT APPOINTMENT! BY GOD, I'M GLAD I SAW THIS WITH MY OWN EYES!
GB Trudeau

SIR, WHAT'D WE HAVE FOR BREAKFAST?
NOTHING SPECIAL. ONE DAY, THIS WILL ALL BE YOURS, HONEY!

FUN, FUN, FUN!
SPANKY, COULD YOU TAKE OVER FOR A MINUTE? I WANT TO GET SOME COFFEE.
SURE, BABE.

WE'LL HAVE FUN, FUN, FUN 'TILL YOUR DADDY TAKES THE... ZWIPP!

YO, RAP HOMES, ICE AND EASY E!... I'M HERE TO DIS THE ATTITUDE THAT WOMEN GOTTA BE... OBJECTS OF CONTEMPT AND MALE BRU-TAL-I-TY! HUNH!
SCRATCH
SCRATCH!!

YOU WANNA TALK SMOKED? MY TRIGGER FINGER ITCHES... WHEN I HEAR THE RAPPIN' FOOLS WHO BE CALLIN' WOMEN "B-----S"! BO! BO! BO!
BAPPITY! BAP! BAP!
SSCRAAATCH!

PLOP!
GBTrudeau

THANKS.
NO CHARGE.
FUN... BIP!
FUN... BIP!
FUN... BIP!

MRS. POCATELLI? IS THAT YOU?
NICE TO SEE YOU AGAIN, JOAN, DEAR!

GOSH, HOW LONG'S IT BEEN?
TOO LONG, DEAR. COME ON IN. ANDY'LL BE THRILLED TO SEE YOU.

HOW'S HE FEELING THESE DAYS?
NOT SO GOOD. HE'S BEEN ASKIN' TO SEE THE DOC A LOT...

I'M HERE ANDY...WHAT IS IT?
I... I... WANT YOU TO BOOK AEROSMITH FOR MY FUNERAL.

WHAT A WONDERFUL SURPRISE, JOANIE!
I KNOW I SHOULD HAVE CALLED FIRST. IS THIS A BAD TIME, ANDY?

NO, NO, THE DOC AND I ARE JUST GOING OVER THE FINAL FUNERAL ARRANGE-MENTS...
RIGHT, WHERE WERE WE? OH, YES, YOU SAID THE WAKE WAS TO BE CATERED BY TRADER VIC'S...

NEVER MIND THAT! WHAT ABOUT THE PALL-BEARERS?
UH... PALL-BEARERS? DID WE DISCUSS PALLBEARERS?

THE CAST OF "CHEERS"! IT WAS MY DYING WISH!
THERE'VE BEEN SEVERAL.

SO, JOANIE... KNOW ANY NEW AIDS JOKES?
OF COURSE NOT. DO YOU?

YEAH, I KNOW ONE, BUT I CAN'T... CAN'T REMEMBER IT... I'M SO TIRED THESE DAYS, JOANIE, SO... VERY... VERY... TIRED...

OH, ANDY, I...

WAIT, I GOT IT! RABBI WALKS INTO AN AIDS CLINIC...
HEARD IT.

LIKE SOMETHING TO DRINK, JOANIE? I HAVE SOME ICED TEA...
THAT'D BE GREAT. WHERE'S THE KITCHEN?

I'LL GET IT FOR YOU. I'M NOT QUITE AS HELPLESS AS I LOOK...
ARE YOU SURE?

NO. BUT I NEED REASONS TO GET OUT OF THAT DAMN BED. I'VE BEEN PRETTY DEPRESSED LATELY. I CAN'T WORK ANYMORE, I'VE GOT INSURANCE PROBLEMS...

ALSO, THINGS JUST HAVEN'T BEEN THE SAME SINCE THE EARTHQUAKE.

WHAT'S UP, MRS. P? IS THAT YOUR SKETCH?
WHAT SKETCH?

MRS. POCATELLI, BEING A FULL-SERVICE LANDLADY, HAS KINDLY AGREED TO CREATE MY SQUARE FOR THE AIDS QUILT PROJECT.

LET ME SEE. WHAT'S IT SAY?

"ANDY LIPPINCOTT, 1945-1990. HE NEVER BOTHERED THE NEIGHBORS."
I'LL NEED MONEY FOR THE FABRIC.

"ANDY LIPPINCOTT, 1945-1990. HE NEVER BOTHERED THE NEIGHBORS." HMM... I DON'T KNOW IF MRS. POCATELLI HAS QUITE CAPTURED ME...

WHY DON'T YOU COMPOSE YOUR OWN EPITAPH FOR THE QUILT?
GOOD IDEA. LET ME DICTATE SOMETHING TO YOU...

"IN LOVING MEMORY OF ANDY LIPPINCOTT, COMMUNITY LEADER, CONSERVATIONIST, AUTHOR, ARTIST, OLYMPIC MEDALIST, AND WINNER OF THE NOBEL PEACE PRIZE!"

YOU CAN GET AWAY WITH THIS?
THERE'S A BACKLOG. THEY NEVER CHECK.

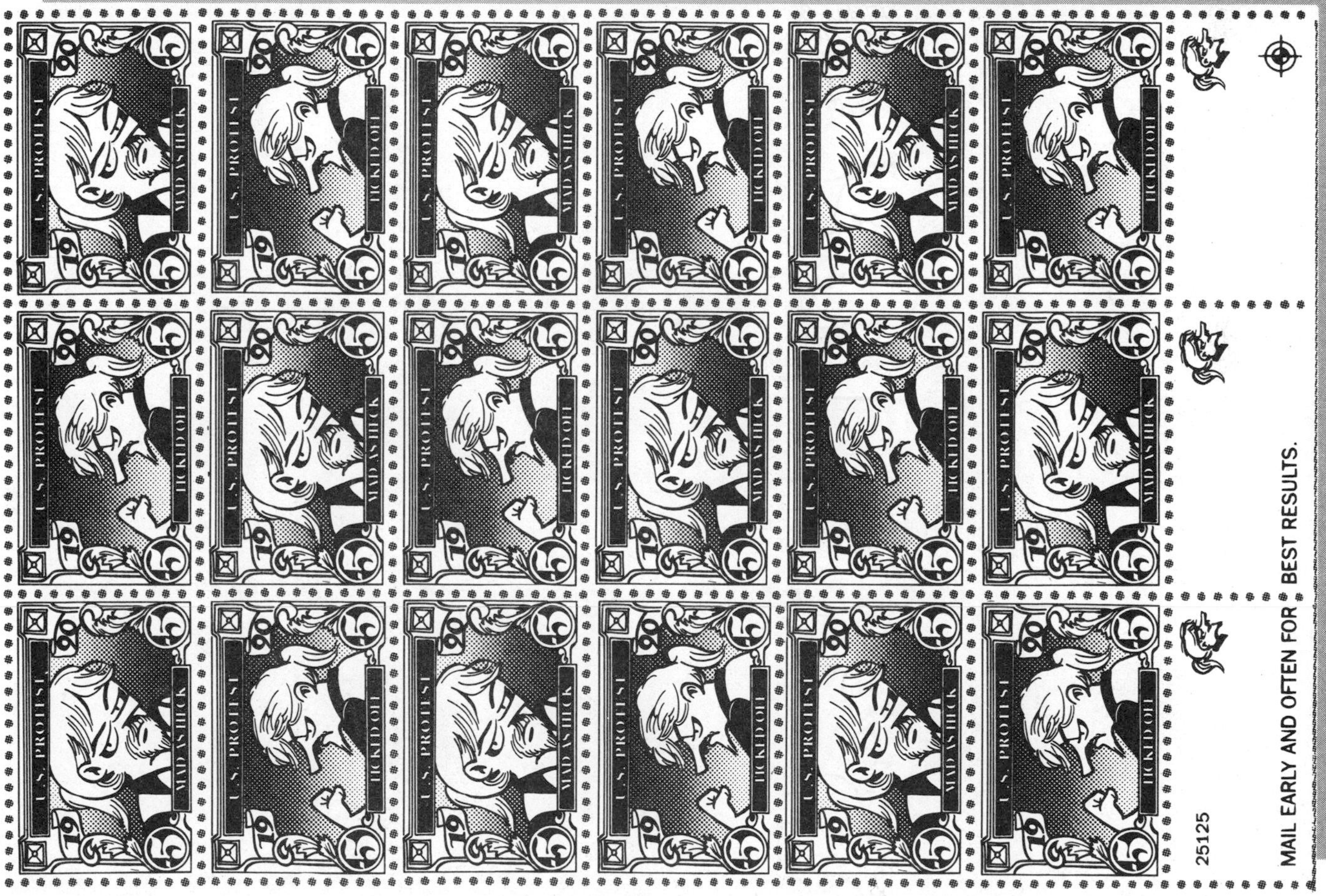

U.S. PROTEST — MAD AS HECK — TICKED OFF

25125

MAIL EARLY AND OFTEN FOR BEST RESULTS.

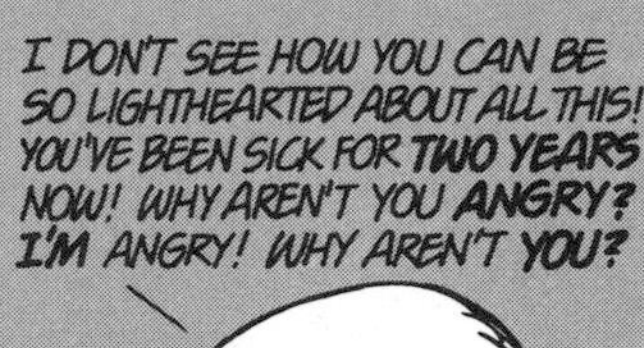

I DID ANGER. IT'S BORING. BESIDES, IT MAKES OTHER PEOPLE UNCOMFORTABLE, AND I **NEED** OTHER PEOPLE.

ANDY, YOU ARE WELL LOVED. YOUR FRIENDS WILL STAND BY YOU NO MATTER **HOW** YOU FEEL!

WHERE'VE YOU BEEN STAYING THIS VISIT, JOANIE? NOT AT A HOTEL, I HOPE.

NO, NO, I'VE BEEN STAYING WITH GINNY SLADE AND HER HUSBAND.
GINNY GOT **MARRIED?** NOT TO THAT MAJOR HOME BOY SHE USED TO HANG WITH?

CLYDE. YUP. BUT HE'S ... WELL ... DIFFERENT NOW.

GOOD **GRAVY,** HON! GEORGE WILL IS RIGHT **AGAIN!**
LUCK.
GBTrudeau

YOU WANT TO TALK ABOUT IT, JOANIE?
TALK ABOUT WHAT?

JOANIE, YOU WERE OVER THERE ALL DAY. HOW'S ANDY DOING?
FINE. INCREDIBLE, HUH? **HE'S** DYING, BUT **I'M** THE BASKET CASE!

TODAY WAS ROUGH. IT ENTAILED LOTS OF ... VIDEOTAPING.
VIDEOTAPING?
YES.
GBTrudeau

LET ME GET YOU SOME MORE WINE.
I'VE GOT TO GET A ROUGH CUT TOGETHER FOR THE FUNERAL.

MAN, I HAD A BAD DAY TODAY!...

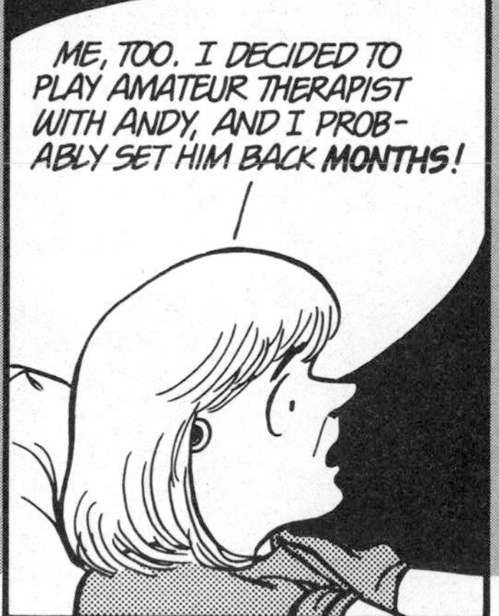
ME, TOO. I DECIDED TO PLAY AMATEUR THERAPIST WITH ANDY, AND I PROBABLY SET HIM BACK **MONTHS**!

I TOLD HIM HE SHOULD BE ANGRY, DESPITE HIS CHOICE NOT TO BE, AND NOW I KNOW HE'S ALL CONFUSED AS TO HOW HE SHOULD COPE AND HOW HE SHOULD FEEL ABOUT DYING! AND IT'S **ALL** MY FAULT!

I'M SORRY. WHAT ABOUT YOUR BAD DAY?
MY PORSCHE BROKE DOWN. YOU ALWAYS HAVE TO TOP PEOPLE, DON'T YOU, BLONDIE?
GBTrudeau

IT WAS FEEDING TIME AT THE VEEP'S OFFICE.
SIR, WHAT'S YOUR ASSESSMENT OF THE CURRENT CONVENTIONAL FORCES NEGOTIATIONS?
UM... DON'T TELL ME...

THE JACKALS WERE CLOSING IN FOR THE KILL.
WHAT'S YOUR POSITION ON ON-SITE INSPECTIONS?
HOW ABOUT OFF-SHORE DRILLING?
OFF-RAMP LOADING?
UM... I'LL HAVE TO GET BACK TO YOU ON THOSE...

IN DESPERATION, DANO REACHED INTO HIS DESK DRAWER...
SIR, WHAT'S THE CAPITAL OF NORTH DAKOTA?
UH...

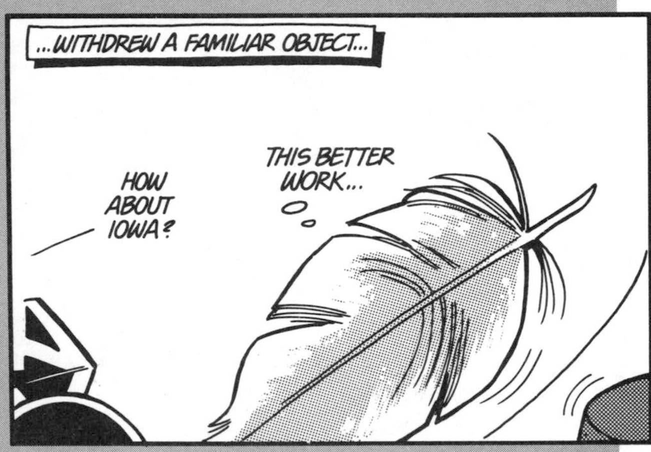
...WITHDREW A FAMILIAR OBJECT...
HOW ABOUT IOWA?
THIS BETTER WORK...

...AND PLACED IT ON THE DESK.
SPROING!
IT WAS PEDRO.

THE CRISIS PASSED.
HA HA! HA! HA!
LOOK AT THAT! HA!
OUTRAGEOUS!
HA! HA!
WHEW...
THWIP!
THWIP!

WHAZZAT, KID?
GUESS. IT'S A LITTLE SOMETHING BY THE BEACH BOYS.

"PET SOUNDS"! ON CD! THEY DID IT! THEY FINALLY RELEASED IT! I LIVED LONG ENOUGH TO HEAR "PET SOUNDS" ON CD!
AND IT'S GOT TWO EXTRA CUTS. I'LL PUT IT ON FOR YOU...

TWO EXTRA CUTS? I TAKE IT BACK! I DIDN'T LIVE LONG ENOUGH! I'VE DIED AND GONE TO HEAVEN!

IN FACT, WHAT ARE YOU DOING HERE?
GOD ONLY KNOWS.
YES. GOD ONLY KNOWS...
GB Trudeau

COULD I EVER FIND IN YOU AGAIN... THINGS THAT MADE ME LOVE YOU SO MUCH THEN...?
WHEW... IT'S INCREDIBLE ON CD!

WHAT A MASTERWORK! DID YOU KNOW "PET SOUNDS" INSPIRED "SERGEANT PEPPER"? DOWN TO THE DETAILS, LIKE THE DOGS BARKING...
OH, CAROLINE, NOOO...

TO THIS DAY, WHENEVER I HEAR THOSE DOGS, I'M TRANSPORTED — JUST OVERWHELMED BY MEMORIES!
OF YOUR FIRST LOVE?

NO, MY FIRST DOG. LISTEN! THAT'S MY LIFE!
WOOF! WOOF! CLANG, CLANG, CLANG!
GB Trudeau

LET'S SEE, I GOT TO HEAR "PET SOUNDS" ON CD, I SAW THE SEASON FINALE OF "L.A. LAW," AND I LIVED TO SEE BUSH RENEGE ON HIS TAX PLEDGE!

PLUS, I MADE MY VIDEO FAREWELL. SO THAT ABOUT COVERS EVERYTHING I WANTED TO DO BEFORE I BIT IT!
BEFORE YOU BIT IT? WHAT ARE YOU TALKING ABOUT?

YOU'VE STILL GOT LOTS TO DO BEFORE YOU... YOU... ANDY?

THE OVEN! I LEFT THE OVEN ON!
I'LL GET IT ON MY WAY OUT. SEE YOU TOMORROW.
GB Trudeau

ANDY, I'M CHECKING THE OVEN BEFORE I GO! IT'S OFF, OKAY? NOTHING TO WORRY ABOUT!

ANDY? DID YOU HEAR ME? ANDY, WILL YOU STOP CUTTING OUT ON ME? IT'S SCARY...

ANDY?
WOULDN'T IT BE NICE...

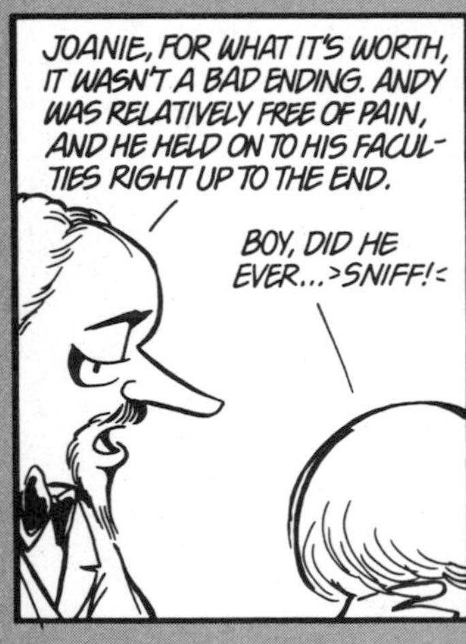
JOANIE, FOR WHAT IT'S WORTH, IT WASN'T A BAD ENDING. ANDY WAS RELATIVELY FREE OF PAIN, AND HE HELD ON TO HIS FACULTIES RIGHT UP TO THE END.
BOY, DID HE EVER... >SNIFF!<

HEY, DOC?
WHAT IS IT, WILLIS?

I FOUND THIS PAD IN ANDY'S HAND. IT LOOKS LIKE HE SCRIBBLED SOMETHING IN IT JUST BEFORE HE DIED.
WHAT'S IT SAY?

"BRIAN WILSON IS GOD."
HMM... HE MUST HAVE GOTTEN HOLD OF THE "PET SOUNDS" CD.

HEY! WHY AREN'T YOU TWO READY? WE'RE GOING TO BE LATE FOR THE GAME! I PAID A FORTUNE FOR THESE TICKETS, AND...
CLYDE, ANDY DIED TODAY.

WHAT?...OH... HEY, I'M SORRY, BLONDIE... THAT'S JUST TERRIBLE... I'M REALLY SORRY TO HEAR THAT...

BUT DON'T YOU THINK ANDY WOULD HAVE WANTED US TO...
CLYDE, GET OUT OF HERE!

ARE YOU COMING TO THE SERVICE, CLYDE?
NO... NO, I HAVE A HARD TIME WITH FUNERALS.

GINNY, HURRY UP! WE'RE GOING TO MISS ANDY'S VIDEO!
COMING! SEE YOU LATER, CLYDE...

VIDEO?

DRY THOSE TEARS, MOURNERS! IT'S TIME FOR STUPID AIDS TRICKS!
OH, NO, NOT THE THING WITH HIS DRIP BOTTLE...

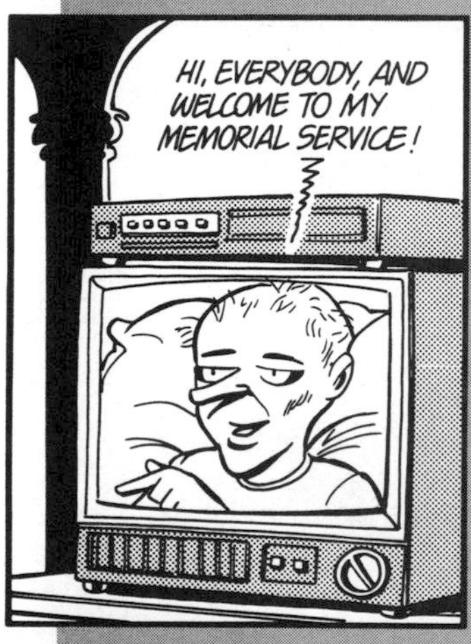
HI, EVERYBODY, AND WELCOME TO MY MEMORIAL SERVICE!

BEFORE WE GET STARTED, I'D JUST LIKE TO ACKNOWLEDGE MY PHYSICIAN, DR. RUDY KLEIN. AIDS IS A BITCH, BUT THIS MAN NEVER LET UP IN TRYING TO KEEP ME ALIVE! TAKE A BOW, RUDY!

IF ANY OF YOU ARE HIV-POSITIVE, I HIGHLY RECOMMEND DR. KLEIN TO YOU! HE IS THE BEST, THE ABSOLUTE BEST!

THANKS, ANDY. I'D JUST LIKE TO SAY...
OF COURSE, HE HAS TO BE! HIS FEES ARE OBSCENE! HA, HA, HA! GOTCHA, DOC!

I WANT TO THANK YOU ALL FOR COMING TO MY MEMORIAL SERVICE...

PLEASE DON'T GET ALL COMPETITIVE WITH YOUR EULOGIES. THIS CHAPEL HAS BEEN BOOKED FOR THE WHOLE DAY, SO THERE'LL BE PLENTY OF TIME FOR EVERYONE TO DO ME JUSTICE!

AND NO WORDS OF PITY, OKAY? I'M DOING FINE NOW. IT'S A LITTLE HARD TO TELL FROM THE DECOR, BUT I THINK I MADE IT INTO HEAVEN!

HEAVEN? INCREDIBLE! THE GUY WAS A LAWYER!
BY THE WAY, JIM HENSON'S HERE.

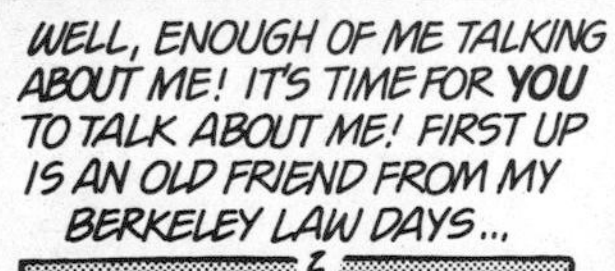
WELL, ENOUGH OF ME TALKING ABOUT ME! IT'S TIME FOR YOU TO TALK ABOUT ME! FIRST UP IS AN OLD FRIEND FROM MY BERKELEY LAW DAYS...

UH-OH... I'M ON...
SHE'S BEEN A REGULAR ANGEL OF MERCY, KIDS! SAY HELLO TO JOANIE CAUCUS! JOANIE?

UM... THANKS, I... SORRY, I CAN'T DO THIS WITHOUT NOTES, AND I... UH... CAN'T SEEM TO FIND THEM... UM... JUST A SEC. THEY'RE IN HERE SOMEWHERE...

GOD, WHERE ARE THEY? MAYBE I LEFT THEM AT HOME... I'M SORRY, I...
THANK YOU, THAT WAS VERY SPECIAL! NEXT UP IS...

THANKS, JOANIE! NEXT UP IS...
HOLD IT, HOLD IT, I'M NOT DONE!
CLIK!
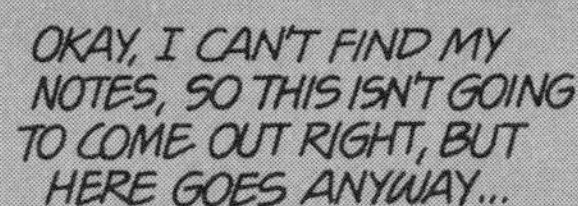
OKAY, I CAN'T FIND MY NOTES, SO THIS ISN'T GOING TO COME OUT RIGHT, BUT HERE GOES ANYWAY...

ANDY LIPPINCOTT WAS THE BRAVEST PERSON I EVER MET. HE DIDN'T SPEND HIS LAST YEAR DYING — HE SPENT IT LIVING. NONE OF US WILL EVER BE THE SAME FOR IT.

WELL, THAT'S ALL I REALLY WANTED TO SAY...
SHE GOT IT RIGHT THE SECOND TIME, DIDN'T SHE?

EXCUSE ME? THAT WAS A LOVELY EULOGY!
OH... THANK YOU.

WOULD YOU MIND IF I ASKED YOU A PERSONAL QUESTION?
WHAT'S THAT?

ARE YOU A TRANSVESTITE?
NO. I'M A MOTHER OF TWO.

A MOTHER OF TWO? WOW... ANDY SURE KNEW SOME INTERESTING PEOPLE!
I'LL SAY.

I THINK ANDY'S PANEL IS UP THERE...

THE QUILT PROJECT HAS GROWN SO IMMENSE. THEY KEEP ADDING PANELS EVERY DAY.

HERE IT IS, LACEY. COME SEE...

ISN'T IT LOVELY? I THINK IT REALLY CAPTURES HIS SPIRIT.

GRACIOUS...

I HAD NO IDEA ANDY WON THE NOBEL PEACE PRIZE.
HE WAS A MODEST MAN, LACEY.

MY, WE'RE UP LATE, JOANIE!

WHA...? WHO ARE YOU?
WHO DO I LOOK LIKE? YOU! AS A YOUNG WOMAN!

YOU...YOU... **CAN'T** BE ME! LOOK AT YOU, YOU'RE... YOU'RE...
I'M WHAT?

YOU'RE **BAREFOOT,** FOR GOD'S SAKE!
THIS IS '67. THE EARTH SHOES CAME LATER.

YOU'RE **ME** 20 YEARS AGO? WHAT ARE YOU **DOING** HERE?
YOU'VE BEEN TRYING TO GET IN TOUCH WITH ME, HAVEN'T YOU?

WELL...YES, I GUESS I HAVE. MY LIFE AS A WORKING MOTHER IS SO MESSY NOW. WHEN I WAS YOU, AT HOME WITH A BABY, IT SEEMED LESS COMPLICATED...
IT WAS NOTHING OF THE KIND. THAT'S WHY YOU LEFT!

≥SIGH≤... I KNOW... BUT I GUESS I'LL ALWAYS WONDER IF I DID THE RIGHT THING...
JOIN THE CLUB.

HEY, LOOK, SINCE YOU'RE HERE, WANNA BAKE SOME BREAD?
ARE YOU NUTS? YOU DIDN'T HAVE TIME **THEN!**

WHY HAVE YOU BEEN TRYING TO GET IN TOUCH WITH ME, JOAN?
I DUNNO. I GUESS YOU REPRESENT A SIMPLER TIME...

WHEN I WAS YOU, I HAD TIME FOR A MORNING CUP OF COFFEE. I WASN'T PREOCCUPIED. I WAS PRESENT FOR MY CHILD. RAISING HER GAVE MY LIFE TANGIBLE PURPOSE...

UM... I DON'T MEAN TO BE RUDE, BUT DO YOU HAVE SOME I.D.?
OKAY, OKAY, MAYBE I'VE ROMANTICIZED IT A BIT...

I STILL HAVEN'T GOT IT RIGHT, JOANIE. AFTER 10 YEARS STAYING AT HOME WITH A CHILD, 9 YEARS WORKING ON A CAREER, AND 7 YEARS COMBINING THE TWO, I **STILL** HAVEN'T A CLUE HOW TO MAKE MY LIFE WORK!

WHAT SORT OF WORK DO YOU DO, JOAN?
I'M A LAWYER.

A LAWYER? YOU'RE A **LAWYER?**
YES. I'M CHIEF COUNSEL FOR A CON-GRESSIONAL COMMITTEE.

RIGHT. AND I'M DATING JIMI HENDRIX.
OH, WOW... I HAD A REAL SELF-ESTEEM PROBLEM, DIDN'T I?

HERE'S THE DEAL, FORMER SELF. WE'RE TALKING CONFLICTED, WE'RE TALKING GUILT, WE'RE TALKING BURN-OUT...

LEAST YOU'RE NOT TALKING BOREDOM...
BOREDOM? I WOULD **WELCOME** BORE-DOM! I WOULD **LOVE** MY LIFE TO BE LESS INTERESTING!

YOU SOUND TIRED, JOANIE GIRL!
TRY EXHAUSTED. THERE'S JUST NO WAY TO HAVE IT ALL, LET ALONE SOME OF IT, ON A FEW HOURS' SLEEP A NIGHT!

I AM WOMAN, HEAR ME **SNORE!**
ARE YOU TIPSY? YOU'RE TIPSY! SEE, I CAN'T **DO** THAT ANYMORE!

JOANIE?
UH... YES, RICK?

WHO ARE YOU TALK-ING TO IN THERE?
UM... NO ONE! I JUST HAVE THE TV ON!

WELL, DON'T STAY UP ALL... **WHOA!** YOU SHOULD SEE THE CAR THAT JUST PULLED UP!
REALLY?
IT LOOKS LIKE A... A... DELOREAN!
OH... THAT'S MY RIDE.

HI. THIS IS ANDY LIPPINCOTT. I'M ACTUALLY DEAD NOW, BUT FROM TIME TO TIME I'LL BE COMING BACK AS A RECURRING DREAM FIGURE.

WHY? BECAUSE LIKE MANY DECEASED FOLKS, I LEFT BEHIND A LOT OF UNFINISHED BUSINESS. LIKE MY BROTHER, FOR INSTANCE. WE NEVER MADE UP. I WANT TO SET THAT STRAIGHT!

AND THE GUYS AT WORK. I NEVER HAD THE CHANCE TO THANK THEM FOR THAT PARTY THEY THREW ME. AND THEN THERE'S STUFF LIKE MY UNPAID VISA BILL, AND THE MESS WITH THE INSURANCE COMPANY. ALL THOSE THINGS NEED TO BE RESOLVED.

WELL, GOTTA RUN FOR NOW. THERE'S A KEVIN COSTNER FANTASY WAITING IN THE WINGS...

THANKS FOR OPENING UP A SLOT, KID. I APPRECIATE THE CHANCE TO...
FINE, FINE. WHERE'S KEVIN?
WHAT?
GB Trudeau

AT ONE TIME, IT SEEMED THERE WAS NO LIMIT TO HIS ACQUISITIVE APPETITES, TO HIS OVERARCHING GREED. MORE THAN ANY OTHER INDIVIDUAL, DONALD J. TRUMP REPRESENTED ALL THAT WAS GROTESQUE ABOUT THE '80s.

SO WHEN THE BILLS CAME DUE LAST FRIDAY, THE MAN WHO HAD ENDLESSLY FLAUNTED HIS EXCESSES FOUND LITTLE SYMPATHY FROM THE PUBLIC HE ONCE CALLED "MY PEOPLE."

REPORTING ON THE DENOUEMENT, LIVE FROM TRUMP TOWER, IS ROLAND HEDLEY...

JUMP! JUMP! JUMP!
PETER, THE EXCITEMENT IS PALPABLE HERE TONIGHT...
©BTrudeau

THIS IS ROLAND HEDLEY, AND WE'RE TALKING TO CURIOUS ONLOOKERS GATHERED OUTSIDE TRUMP TOWER...

MA'AM, WHAT DREW YOU DOWN HERE TODAY?
I JUST COULDN'T STAY AWAY. NORMALLY, I'D FEEL KINDA SMALL GLOATING OVER SOMEONE'S MISFORTUNES...

BUT WITH TRUMP, IT'S DIFFERENT. HE BEGGED FOR IT. HE'S A TRULY OBNOXIOUS HUMAN BEING, AND I THINK IT'S JUST GREAT THAT HIS WHOLE WORLD SEEMS TO BE COLLAPSING!

SO BASICALLY, YOU CAME OUT TO WISH HIM THE WORST.
SURE! MY WHOLE FAMILY DID!
WE EVEN BROUGHT A PICNIC!
©BTrudeau

PETER, AS TRUMP SCRAMBLES TO CROSS-COLLATERALIZE, 65 FLOORS BELOW HIM, CURIOUS LOCALS HAVE GATHERED ON THE STREET! TELL ME, SIR—WHAT WILL YOU MISS MOST ABOUT THE DONALD'S LIFESTYLE?

HARD TO SAY. THERE'S SO MUCH THAT'S REPELLENT ABOUT THE GUY. THE BOASTING, THE PIGGISH CONSUMPTION, THE SQUALID PERSONAL LIFE...
HOW ABOUT THE HIDEOUS DECOR OF HIS CASINOS?

NAH, WHO CARES ABOUT DECOR? HIS SQUALID PERSONAL LIFE WAS THE MOST OFFENSIVE THING ABOUT HIM!
IT WAS NOT! THE WORST WAS THE HIDEOUS DECOR!

HIS SQUALID PERSONAL LIFE!
THE HIDEOUS DECOR!
HIS PERSONAL LIFE!
NEW YAWKAHS! THEY NEVER AGREE! WHAT ARE YOU GONNA DO, PETER?
©BTrudeau

TOMMY MANDEL, AS A TRUMP TOWER DOORMAN, YOU WERE ONE OF TRUMP'S LITTLE PEOPLE. WHAT WAS THAT LIKE?
A MAJOR PAIN, I'LL TELL YOU THAT.

TRUMP PUT IN HIS OFFICIAL RESUMÉ THAT HE WAS "A MAN OF THE PEOPLE" BECAUSE HE TALKED TO HIS DOORMEN ON HIS WAY OUT EVERY DAY! CAN YOU BELIEVE THAT CRAPOLA?

WELL, THE SHOE'S ON THE OTHER FOOT NOW! EVER SINCE I SEEN ALL THOSE BANKERS PARADIN' IN AND OUTA HERE, I AIN'T GIVEN TRUMP THE TIME OF DAY!

BUT DON'T YOU... FEAR FOR YOUR JOB?
NAH. I'M REAL NICE TO THE BANKERS.
©B Trudeau

PETER, I'M NOW TALKING TO AN ACTUAL HOMELESS PERSON IN THE SOARING ATRIUM OF THE TRUMP TOWER...
YEAH, I JUST WANNA SAY ONE THING!

THEY SAY TRUMP RAISED $1 BILLION TO BUILD THE TAJ. WELL, $1 BILLION COULD PROVIDE PERMANENT HOUSING FOR EVERY HOMELESS FAMILY IN NEW YORK CITY...

THINK OF THE GOOD THAT A MAN WITH HIS RESOURCES AND CLOUT COULDA DONE! THINK OF THE DIFFERENCE HE COULDA MADE! WHAT A WASTE!

SO YOU'RE HERE TO BEAR WITNESS?
NO, ACTUALLY, I LIVE HERE. IN THE BANK-MACHINE LOBBY.
©B Trudeau

MR. CHAIRMAN, I WOULD ADDRESS MY OPENING REMARKS TO THE TASK FORCE'S NEXT WITNESS, HERE TO TESTIFY ON BEHALF OF THE TOBACCO INSTITUTE...

WE'VE HAD QUITE A PARADE OF INDUSTRY SPOKESPERSONS COME THROUGH HERE THIS WEEK TO DENOUNCE OUR PROPOSED BAN ON TOBACCO ADVERTISING...

BUT **YOU**, SIR — YOU ARE THE VERY **EMBODIMENT** OF A PUBLIC HEALTH PROBLEM OF VAST, TRAGIC DIMENSIONS!

I TRY. YOU'RE VERY KIND.
©B Trudeau

MY NAME? **MR. BUTTS**, OF COURSE!
DO YOU SWEAR TO TELL THE TRUTH, THE WHOLE TRUTH, AND NOTHING BUT THE TRUTH, SO HELP YOU GOD?

I DO!
PLEASE BE SEATED.

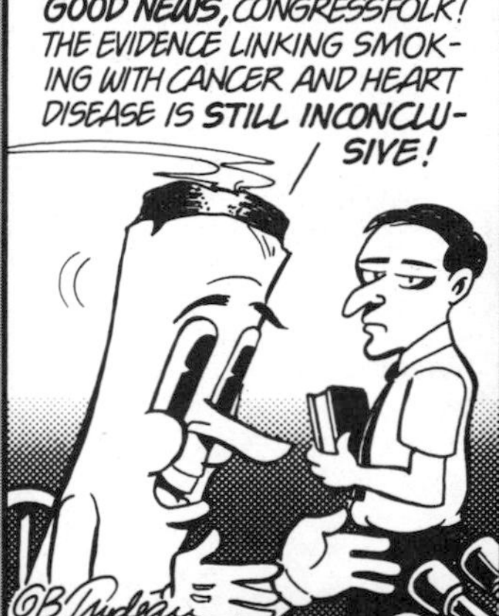
GOOD NEWS, CONGRESSFOLK! THE EVIDENCE LINKING SMOKING WITH CANCER AND HEART DISEASE IS **STILL INCONCLUSIVE**!
©B Trudeau

I DON'T KNOW WHY I EVEN BOTHER...
THAT'S RIGHT, THE JURY IS **STILL OUT**! IS THAT **GREAT** OR **WHAT**?

RIVETING NEWS, LAWMAKERS! THE CASE AGAINST SMOKING IS **STILL** IN DISPUTE! CALL OFF YOUR ADVERTISING BAN!

THE BAN IS UNCONSTITUTIONAL ANYWAY! PEOPLE HAVE A **RIGHT** TO KNOW WHICH IMAGE THEIR CIGARETTE BRAND PROJECTS!

THE BAN WILL BRING **CHAOS**! COWBOYS WILL START SMOKING VIRGINIA SLIMS! BLACKS WILL SMOKE WHITE BRANDS! YOU CAN'T... >HACK!< YOU CAN'T **DO**... >COUGH!< THIS!

WOULD THE WITNESS LIKE A RECESS TO PULL HIMSELF TOGETHER?
PLEASE.
©B Trudeau

For people who like to smoke...

SURGEON GENERAL'S WARNING: Cigarette Smoke Contains Carbon Monoxide.

EVEN HIS TOUGHEST CRITICS HAVE TO CONCEDE HIS PHENOMENAL POPULARITY AS A LEADER.
IS HE IN? YES, I'LL HOLD.

HE IS MORE POPULAR WITH AMERICANS THAN ANY PAST PRESIDENT EVER WAS, INCLUDING REAGAN.

SURE, THERE'VE BEEN SOME PROBLEMS ON HIS WATCH—AN UNCOMPETITIVE ECONOMY, GROWING ENVIRONMENTAL CONCERNS, A SOARING CRIME RATE, PERSISTENT HOMELESSNESS...

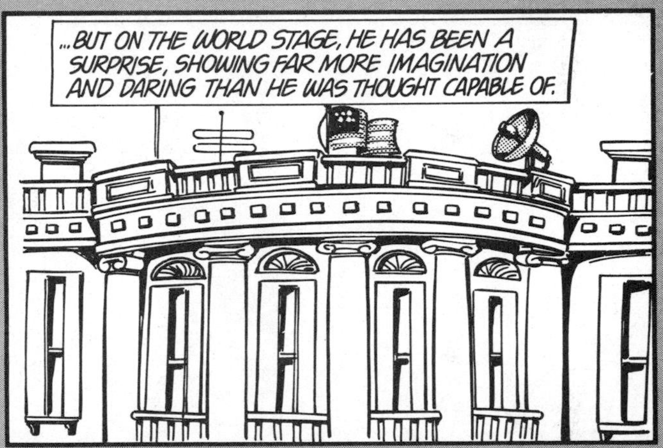
...BUT ON THE WORLD STAGE, HE HAS BEEN A SURPRISE, SHOWING FAR MORE IMAGINATION AND DARING THAN HE WAS THOUGHT CAPABLE OF.

HE IS KNOWLEDGEABLE ON A WIDE RANGE OF FOREIGN POLICY ISSUES, HE IS A SHREWD NEGOTIATOR...

...AND HE TALKS REGULARLY WITH GEORGE BUSH!
GORBY? IT'S ME! UH... SURE... I CAN HOLD A LITTLE LONGER...
GBTrudeau

MIKE, THESE NEW LAYOUTS ARE SUPERB! I THINK YOU'RE READY FOR A NEW CLIENT OF OURS.
WHO'S THAT, MR. BEL-LOWS?

TERMEX. THEY MAKE INSECTICIDE SPRAYS. THEY'RE INVOLVED IN SOME MESSY LITIGATION RIGHT NOW, AND THEY NEED AN IMAGE MAKE-OVER. WHAT DO YOU SAY?

UH...WELL, SIR, IF THAT'S WHAT YOU'D LIKE ME TO DO, I SUP-POSE I...UH...
I QUIT!

I SENSE SOME AMBIVA-LENCE...
ME, TOO.

SURE, MR. BELLOWS, I'LL TAKE THE INSEC-TICIDE ACCOUNT...
THAT DOES IT! I QUIT!
ARE YOU SURE?

UH...NO PROB-LEM.
NO WAY! I'M OUTA HERE! I'M HISTORY!
WHY DON'T YOU SLEEP ON IT...

SLEEP ON IT?
WHY DON'T YOU SIT ON IT! I'M JOINING THE PEACE CORPS!
WELL, YOU SEEM A LITTLE TENTATIVE.

THE HELL I AM! I HATE BUGS!
OH. THEN YOU'LL DO IT?

IT WAS WEIRD, J.J.! EVEN WHILE MY MOUTH WAS AC-CEPTING THE JOB, EMOTION-ALLY, I WAS CLEANING OUT MY DESK!

IT WAS LIKE SOME PART OF ME WAS OVERCOME WITH REVULSION, AND JUST UP AND QUIT! I MEAN, I'M STILL DRAWING A SALARY, BUT THAT PART IS OUT THE DOOR! HE'S GONE!

I SEE. AND WHAT'S HE DOING NOW?
WELL, THAT'S WHERE IT GETS REAL STRANGE. HE JOINED THE PEACE CORPS.

NEWLY SINGLE, IS HE?
NO, NO, HIS WIFE TEACHES ANIMAL HUSBANDRY.

I DUNNO, J.J., MAYBE I SHOULD LISTEN TO MY INNER VOICE...

MAYBE IT **IS** TIME TO QUIT THE BUSINESS AND FIND MORE SATIS-FYING WORK...

MIKE, ENOUGH WITH THE VOICES. YOU HAVE A FAMILY. AS WEIRD AS IT MAY SOUND COMING FROM ME, YOU HAVE RESPON-SIBILITIES.

I KNOW... YOU'RE RIGHT.
I WANT A DIVORCE.
'NIGHT.
©B Trudeau

MIKE, NO MATTER WHAT YOUR LITTLE VOICES TELL YOU, YOU MUST PROMISE ME YOU WILL NEVER, EVER SERIOUSLY CONSIDER JOINING THE PEACE CORPS.

AGREED.
GOOD.

IS THE BANANA REPUBLIC OPEN LATE TONIGHT?

NO!
WHAT? I DIDN'T TOUCH YOU.
©B Trudeau

MR. BELLOWS, I HAVE TO SPEAK WITH YOU. IT'S IMPORTANT...
YOU KNOW, I FEEL MELLOWER TODAY...

AGAINST MY BETTER JUDG-MENT, AND OVER MY WIFE'S PROTEST...,
WHY ALL THE FUSS OVER ONE STUPID ACCOUNT?

I QUIT.
I THINK I'LL STAY.
©B Trudeau

WHAT?
UM...JUST KIDDING!
ASK FOR A RAISE.

WHO YOU WATCHING, DAD?

THAT'S RICHARD NIXON, SON. A LONG TIME AGO, HE WAS OUR PRESIDENT.

OH...

LOOK... JEFF'S ABSOLUTELY MESMERIZED!
DOESN'T THAT TAKE YOU BACK?

HE'S LYING RIGHT NOW, ISN'T HE?
O, FRESH EYES!
A NEW GENERATION RECOILS!
©B Trudeau

HEY, SWEET THANG. HOW'S IT GOING?
FINE. WANT SOME SMOKE?
02-18-79
20:80:07

YOU KNOW WHAT I WANT, HONEY.
PASS. COULD YOU SPEAK UP?
12-18-79
20:20:01

WHY? WHAT'S GOING ON?
NOTHING. RELAX. DON'T BE SO SUSPICIOUS.
02-18-79
20:20:05

PUFF! PUFF!
YOU'RE RIGHT. I NEED TO UNWIND. WANT SOME?
NO THANKS. I GOTTA GO.
02-19-80
20:80:00

FBI, MR. AMBASSA-DOR!
WHAT? I'VE BEEN SET UP!
ASSUME THE POSITION, EXCELLENCY!
FBI
02-18-80
20:28:04

HEE, HEE! FORTUNATELY, THEY FORGOT TO READ ME MY RIGHTS!
PSST! SIR! THE GUESTS ARE NODDING OFF!

B.D., I THINK HUNK-RA WANTS TO SPEAK TO YOU...
JUST MY LUCK.

HEY! DRAGON-DUNG! ENOUGH DECADENT CO-HABITATING WITH YOUR LADY FRIEND! EITHER MARRY HER...

...OR PEDDLE HER LIKE A SLAB OF HALIBUT ON THE OPEN FLESH MARKET!
GB Trudeau

WHAT'D HE SAY?
HE THINKS I SHOULD GET YOU A STUDIO DEAL.

WHATCHA THINKIN' ABOUT, BABE?
HUNK-RA. WHAT HE REALLY TOLD ME WAS THAT WE SHOULD GET MARRIED. I THINK HE'S RIGHT.

WHY, B.D.! ARE YOU ASKING ME TO MARRY YOU? YOU ARE! RIGHT HERE ON MALIBU BEACH! LIKE OUT OF A MADE-FOR-TV MOVIE!
I THINK JOHNNY CARSON ASKED HIS THIRD WIFE HERE!

I CAN'T STAND IT! AFTER ALL THESE YEARS! OH, B.D., LET'S DREAM, LET'S PLAN!
OKAY. WHERE DO WE START?

THE PRESS RELEASE! IT HAS TO BE TASTEFUL!
LEAVE IT TO ME, SWEET CHEEKS!
GB Trudeau

YOU DON'T LIKE THE PRESS RE-LEASE? WHAT'S WRONG WITH IT?
TRY READING IT OUT LOUD.

"MISS BARBARA ANN BOOPSTEIN, ACCLAIMED ACTRESS, VOCAL STYLIST AND CHANNELER, ANNOUNCES HER ENGAGEMENT TO HER MANAGER."

YOUR NAME. YOU'D LIKE YOUR NAME.
UNLESS YOU THINK IT'D DETRACT!
GB Trudeau

HOW'S THAT WORK, B.D.?
SIMPLE. FIRST I ENTER THE FAX NUMBERS OF ALL THE BIG MEDIA OUTLETS...

THEN I PUT IN OUR ENGAGEMENT ANNOUNCEMENT, HIT THE TRANSMIT BUTTON, AND BINGO—OUR NEWS BELONGS TO THE **WORLD**!
WHIRRR!

WHIRR!
WHIRRR!
WHIRRR!

I FEEL SO NAKED.
LET'S SEE HOW THEY PLAY IT ON THE TUBE.
GB Trudeau

WELL, CONGRATULATIONS, BOOPSIE! ALL I CAN SAY IS IT'S ABOUT **TIME**!
IT JUST FINALLY SEEMED LIKE THE RIGHT MOMENT, MIKE!

HAVE YOU TOLD YOUR PARENTS YET?
OF COURSE! THEY WERE THE FIRST PEOPLE WE FAXED!

"FAXED"?

WHAT IS IT, DEAR?
A PRESS RELEASE. FROM OUR DAUGHTER.
GB Trudeau

THE WIRES ARE BURNING TODAY, EH, JER?
WELL, IT'S JUNK FAX, MOSTLY...
WHIRR!
WHIRR!
WHIRR!

"BARBARA BOOPSTEIN AND HER MANAGER B.D. ANNOUNCE THEIR ENGAGEMENT. MEDIA INQUIRIES WELCOME."
WE MUST GET 50 OF THOSE A DAY.

MIND IF I ANSWER THIS ONE?
BE MY GUEST.

"WHO **ARE** YOU?"
MUST BE A CRANK.
GB Trudeau

SID? BOOPSIE! PACK YOUR BAG, WE'RE GOING TO LAS VEGAS!
WHAT, NO BIG WEDDING?

IT WAS TURNING INTO A MAJOR HASSLE. WE WANT SOMETHING SIMPLE. CAN YOU BE READY IN AN HOUR?
UH...SURE. BOOPSIE, HAVE YOU TOLD YOUR PARENTS?

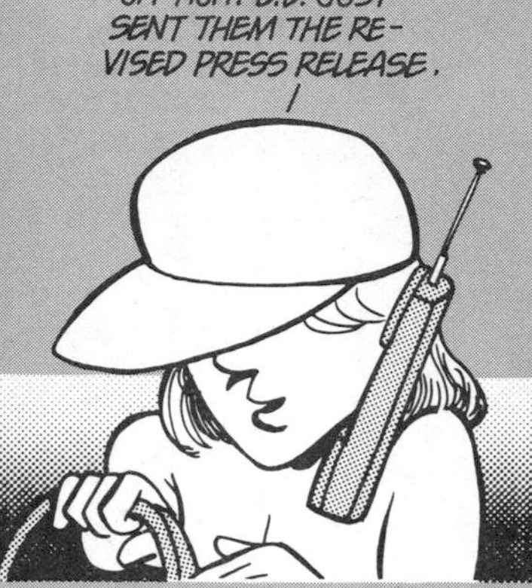
UH-HUH. B.D. JUST SENT THEM THE RE-VISED PRESS RELEASE.

WHAT'S IT SAY? WHAT'S IT SAY?
GOOD NEWS. I'M NOT PAY-ING FOR IT.
GB Trudeau

CAN I BELIEVE YOU KIDS! TEN MINUTES' NOTICE, AND WE'RE OFF TO VEGAS? THE JOCK AND THE STAR, TOOLING OFF INTO THE UNKNOWN! ROAD MOVIE CITY!
80

NOW, YOU STOP THAT, SID! B.D. AND I WON'T LET YOU PACK-AGE OUR STORY! WE VALUE OUR PRIVACY MUCH TOO MUCH!
I READ YOU, BABE. A MAJOR THEATRICAL RELEASE IS OUT OF BOUNDS!

OF COURSE, WE ARE PUBLIC FIGURES.
ARE YOU THINKING DISNEY, SID?
NAH. TOO RAW FOR DISNEY.
GB Trudeau

YES, THIS IS MISS BOOPSTEIN IN 1612. I'M WONDERING IF YOU COULD REC-OMMEND A NICE CHAPEL TO ME...
FOUND ONE!

YOU DID? WHERE?
IN THE PAPER. LISTEN TO THIS...

"HOWDY, PARDNERS! COME ON DOWN AND DO THE DEED IN AIR-CON-DITIONED COMFORT! ROOTIN', TOOTIN' NUPTIALS WITH VALET PARKIN', ALL FOR $39.95! ONLY AT THE HITCHIN' POST CHAPEL!"

GEE, I DUNNO, B.D...
C'MON, IT'S PERFECT! IT EVEN COMES WITH A STEAK DINNER!
WITH SLAW! I LOVE SLAW!
GB Trudeau

ANOTHER WEDDING UPDATE JUST CAME OVER THE FAX, MIKE.
LET'S SEE...

"MISS BARBARA ANN BOOPSTEIN AND HER MANAGER B.D. WILL BE MARRIED TODAY IN A PRIVATE CEREMONY AT LAS VEGAS' HITCHIN' POST CHAPEL."

"HITCHIN' POST CHAPEL"?
©B Trudeau

BEST MAN? HOW'D YA WANT THAT STEAK?
STILL TWITCHING, PADRE!

HEY, LISTEN, BEFORE YOU KIDS TIE THE BIG KNOT, LET ME LAY A WEDDING PRESENT ON YOU!
5¢

AW, SID...
AS YOU KNOW, I'VE BEEN STRAIGHT FOR OVER A YEAR NOW, SO I WANTED YOU TO HAVE THIS FOR YOUR HONEYMOON! ENJOY!

SID, YOU ARE SO THOUGHTFUL! LOOK, B.D., IT'S A BOX FULL OF... OF... UM...

PRESCRIPTION DRUGS?
KIND OF A GRAB BAG. A FEW DATES MAY HAVE EXPIRED...
©B Trudeau

OKAY, WHILE THE BEST MAN FINISHES HIS STEAK, WHY DON'T WE START THIS HERE CEREMONY?
GO TO IT, PADRE.

DEARLY BELOVED, WE ARE GATHERED HERE TO...
TAKE A HIKE, COWBOY, OR I, HUNK-RA, WILL FEED YOU YOUR ENTRAILS!

OKAY, WHAT JUST HAPPENED?
OH... DID WE HAVE A LITTLE VISITOR?
WE HAD A LITTLE VISITOR.
©B Trudeau

UH... LISTEN, MISS, COULD YOU KEEP THE NUTSY STUFF UNDER CONTROL UNTIL I FINISH THE SERVICE?
HOW DARE YOU?

I AM LORD HUNK-RA, SUPREME RULER OF THE GREATER BABYLON AREA, AND PARTS OF THE GAZA STRIP! CAPICHE?

FOR 20,000 YEARS, I HAVE CARRIED THE DIVINE SPARK OF THE CREATOR WITHIN MY BREAST! I SHALL PERFORM THIS CEREMONY!
GB Trudeau

SUIT YOURSELF.
WHAT, WHAT?
HUNK JUST PULLED RANK.
HEY, PADRE! GOT ANY A-1 SAUCE?

DO YOU, B.D., TAKE THE WENCH BOOPSIE TO HAVE AND TO BREED WITH 'TIL...
HOLD IT. I NEVER GOT YOU AN ENGAGEMENT RING!

AN ENGAGEMENT RING? OH, B.D., YOU DON'T HAVE TO GET ME AN ENGAGEMENT RING!
OF COURSE I DO. HEY, PADRE, ANY JEWELRY STORES NEAR HERE?

YEAH. "WILD BILL'S RING SHACK." IT'S ACROSS THE STREET!
JUST A LITTLE ONE, THEN! WITH JUST A TEENY-WEENY DIAMOND...

...LIKE, ABOUT THE SIZE OF GIBRALTAR!
BACK OFF, HUNK.
GB Trudeau

HE SURE IS TAKING A LONG TIME PICKING OUT THAT RING, KID...

MAYBE THEY DIDN'T HAVE A BIG ENOUGH ONE AT "WILD BILL'S RING SHACK."
THAT MUST BE IT. HE MUST BE SHOPPING AROUND...

SO WHERE'RE YOU FOLKS AIMIN' TO SETTLE DOWN— HERE IN LAS VEGAS?
NO, NO, MALIBU. IT'S THE ONLY PLACE WE COULD EVER LIVE!

WHERE TO, SON?
NEW YORK.
Coors
ACE
TRU
GB Trudeau

WHAT ARE YOU AND YOUR FRIENDS SAYING ABOUT BUSH NOW, DEAR?
WHO?
TYPICAL. HOW PATHETIC.

HEY, TWENTY-SOMETHINGS! IS THAT YOU—ALWAYS UNINFORMED 'CAUSE YOU DON'T READ THE PAPERS?

STOP EMBARRASSING YOURSELF AROUND YOUR ELDERS! CATCH UP WITH MY SPECIAL PRIMER ON THE BIG ISSUES OF TODAY!

LET'S START WITH THE COLD WAR, OKAY? HERE'S THE DEAL—IT'S OVER, AND WE WON!

IN SOUTH AFRICA, ON THE OTHER HANDS, FOLKS STILL DON'T GET ALONG! KEEP AN EYE ON MANDELA—HE'S KEY!

THE MID-EAST CRISIS: THE JEWS AND ARABS HAVE BEEN KILLING EACH OTHER OVER THIS GOD-FORSAKEN REAL ESTATE FOR CENTURIES! THEY STILL ARE.

DOMESTICALLY, THERE'S THE S+L CRISIS! HARD TO GRASP, BUT FOR THOSE AMERICANS WHO CAN STILL COUNT, IT'S GOING TO COST ABOUT $500 BILLION!
FIRST SAVING

AND THEN THERE'S YOUR PRESIDENT! HE HAD ONLY ONE CONVICTION—NO TAXES—BUT NOW HE HAS NONE! WITH GEORGE BUSH, YOU AIN'T SEEN NOTHIN' YET—NOR WILL YOU!

WELL, THAT'S IT! A BIG-ISSUE ROUNDUP! READ 'EM AGAIN, AND YOU'LL BE READY TO HIT THE DINNER TABLE! GOOD LUCK!

HEY, DAD! I KNOW WHO GREG BUSH IS!
NO, YOU DON'T.
GB Trudeau

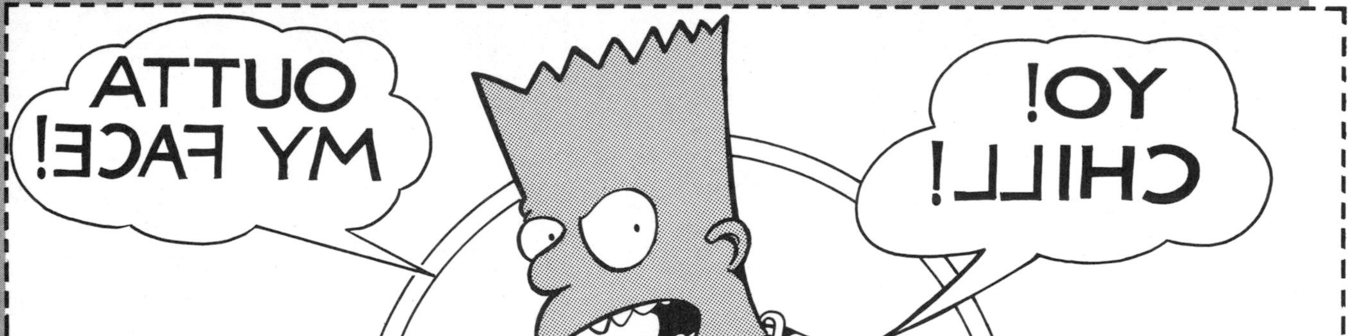

OUTTA MY FACE!

YO! CHILL!

MC BS-KOW

GB Trudeau

MICHAEL! IS THAT YOU? GUESS WHAT I BROUGHT HOME TODAY!
UH... J.J. ...

I BROUGHT HOME A NEW IDEA FOR A PERFORMANCE PIECE SO TRUTHFUL, SO INNOVATIVE, THAT THE NATIONAL ENDOWMENT WILL **HAVE** TO RECONSIDER MY GRANT APPLICATION!

IN FACT, IF I EXPLAINED MY CONCEPT TO JESSE HELMS HIMSELF, EVEN **HE** WOULD HAVE TO CONCEDE THAT **THIS** IS WHAT SUBSIDIZED ART IS ALL ABOUT!

SO WHAT DID **YOU** BRING HOME?
SOME GUYS FROM THE OFFICE.
HI.
WE GOTTA RUN.

OKAY, THIS IS THE NEW CONCEPT FOR MY PERFORMANCE PIECE... READY?
YUP. ON WITH THE SHOW!

LUBRICANTS ON PARADE! CONDOS, SLIPPERY WITH **SPITTLE!** CRANKCASES, CRACKED, OOZING HOT, VISCOUS JUICES! A TALL WOMAN SCREAMS AT NIXON! THE PAIN PASSES...

OH, NO... NO, NO, **NO!** WHAT AM I **DOING?**
WHAT? WHAT'S THE PROBLEM?

DON'T YOU **SEE?** I'M **CENSORING** MYSELF! JUST TO GET THE **GRANT!**
IT DID SEEM A LITTLE MAINSTREAM.

YOU SEE WHAT I'M **DOING,** MIKE? I'M **EDITING** MYSELF! I'VE BEEN UNCONSCIOUSLY COMPROMISING THE PIECE TO MAKE IT MORE ACCEPTABLE TO THE N.E.A.!

THAT'S THE TERRIBLE FALL-OUT WHEN ARTISTS TRY TO PLEASE THE GOVERNMENT—SELF-CENSORSHIP! SAFE ART!
AND YOU THINK YOU WERE TURNED DOWN BECAUSE YOUR PIECE WAS CONSIDERED DANGEROUS?

I'M SURE OF IT! IT WAS EITHER THAT OR BECAUSE OF THE ENDING. I REFUSED TO SCALE BACK THE PRODUCTION VALUES, SO IT MAY HAVE COST TOO MUCH.
WHAT HAPPENS IN THE ENDING?

I BURN 3,000 AMERICAN FLAGS.
YEAH, IT MUST HAVE COST TOO MUCH.

YOU KNOW, J.J., I DOUBT THE N.E.A. RECONSIDERS GRANTS NO MATTER **WHAT** THE CHANGES...
BZZZ!

WAS THAT THE DOOR?
YEAH, I GOT IT.

NO, I'LL... J.J.!

YES?
NOT NOW, J.J.! WHERE'S MIKE?

...AND THEN HUNK-RA TOOK OVER AGAIN! BOOPSIE FELL DOWN ON ALL FOURS AND STARTED BARKING. THAT'S WHEN I BOLTED.

I JUST COULDN'T GO THROUGH WITH IT! I MEAN, CAN YOU IMAGINE BEING MARRIED TO SOMEONE **THAT** OUT OF CONTROL?

HEY, YOU MUST BE **FAMISHED!**
ANSWER THE QUESTION.

YOU MEAN, YOU DIDN'T EVEN SAY GOODBYE TO BOOPSIE?
HOW COULD I? HUNK WOULDN'T LET ME TALK TO HER!

HAVE YOU CALLED HER SINCE? OF COURSE YOU HAVE. ONLY AN UNFEELING BRUTE...
GET OUTTA MY FACE, WILLYA, HARRIS? THIS IS **NONE** OF YOUR BUSINESS!

POOR BOOPSIE! NOT EVEN A CALL! I BET SHE'S HOME NOW, WALKING THE BEACH, SOBBING HER EYES OUT OVER YOU...

NOBODY DUMPS LORD HUNK-RA! **NOBODY!**

CALL HER? NO **WAY** I'M CALLING HER, MIKE! I MIGHT GET HUNK ON THE PHONE...
DONG DONG!

I'LL GET IT.
B.D., THAT'S JUST AVOIDING THE ISSUE. SOONER OR LATER, YOU'RE GOING TO HAVE TO GO HOME AND FACE BOOPSIE.

LOOK, MIKE, I KNOW YOU'D LIKE ME OUT OF YOUR APARTMENT, BUT...
NOW, B.D., I DIDN'T SAY THAT. WHO IS IT, J.J.?

I'VE LOST MY JOB.
ANOTHER PATIENT!

B.D., I AM **NOT** TRYING TO GET RID OF YOU! BUT I JUST DON'T SEE HOW YOU CAN RESOLVE YOUR PROBLEMS WITH BOOPSIE BY SITTING AROUND **HERE!**
MIKE?

JOANIE! WHAT A NICE SURPRISE!
MIKE, FORGIVE ME FOR BARGING IN, BUT I'M GOING THROUGH A BIT OF A CRISIS, AND I HAD TO TALK WITH J.J....

OF COURSE, JOANIE. I HOPE YOU'LL STAY AS LONG AS YOU LIKE.
YOU PROMISE YOU'RE NOT TOO UPSET WITH ME?
DON'T BE SILLY! LET ME TAKE THAT BAG!

WHO LET YOU IN?
UM... J.J. DID. SEE, YOU **ARE** UPSET.
NO, HE'S ALWAYS LIKE THIS!

HELLO?
HI, BABY, IT'S ME. THANK GOD YOU'RE OKAY! I'VE BEEN SO WORRIED!
SURE, SURE...

MIKE CALLED AND EXPLAINED THE WHOLE THING! BABE, I HAD NO IDEA HUNK HAD BEEN CAUSING SUCH PROBLEMS! I FEEL AWFUL!

I'M ASKING HIM TO LEAVE, B.D.! PERMANENTLY, THIS TIME! NO MORE HUNK! JUST YOU AND ME! WHAT DO YOU SAY, BABY? WILL YOU GIVE ME ONE LAST CHANCE?

FIRE UP THE JACUZZI, KID! I'M COMIN' HOME!
SNARF!
SNARF?

BOOPSIE! OVER HERE!
38

HI, KIDDO!
HI, BABE! SORRY I'M LATE! I GOT STOPPED BY THE METAL DE-TECTOR!

THE METAL DETEC-TOR?
YEAH. I THINK IT WAS PICKING UP HUNK'S BREASTPLATE.
GB Trudeau

HUNK? YOU SAID HE WAS...
HE'S GONE, B.D.! I PRO-MISE! HE JUST HASN'T CLEANED OUT HIS LOCKER!

IT WASN'T THE THOUGHT OF MARRYING YOU THAT SPOOKED ME, BOOPSIE— IT WAS THE PACKAGE DEAL! HUNK-RA WAS GETTING OUT OF CON-TROL!

ALL THAT SCREAMING AT THE MIN-ISTER, THE DROOLING, THE... WHAT ARE YOU DO-ING?
HOLD THAT THOUGHT, BABY. I HAVE TO MAKE A CALL.

BURRR!

HELLO?
I'M SORRY.
GB Trudeau

MIKE, I'VE DECIDED NOT TO APPLY FOR ANY MORE N.E.A. GRANTS...

NO? WHY NOT?
BECAUSE A FEDERALLY SUBSIDIZED AVANT-GARDE IS A CONTRADICTION IN TERMS. THE ORIGINAL AVANT-GARDE MOVEMENT WAS CREATED TO BREAK **AWAY** FROM OFFICIALLY SANCTIONED ART! IT'S TIME WE GOT BACK TO OUR ROOTS!

INSTEAD OF DEMANDING SUPPORT FROM THE FEDS, I'M GOING TO CREATE A PERFORMANCE PIECE THAT SPITS IN THEIR FACES! I'M GOING TO WRITE A SHOW SO OFFENSIVE, SO INCENDIARY, THEY CAN'T IGNORE ME!

THEN I'LL TAKE IT TO CINCINNATI, WHERE THEY'LL HAVE TO ARREST ME AND SEND ME TO JAIL, WHERE I'LL CONDUCT A SERIES OF HUNGER STRIKES! IT'LL BE A **KILLER** PIECE, AN **INCREDIBLY** BOLD TWO-YEAR STATEMENT!

UH... TWO YEARS? YOU'LL BE GONE FOR TWO YEARS?
LONGER, MAYBE. DEPENDS ON MY SENTENCE.

AND WHO'S GOING TO TAKE CARE OF THE KID?
WHO TAKES CARE OF HER NOW?
I DO, BUT I DON'T WORK FOR FELONS.
GBTrudeau

COULD I HAVE EVERYONE'S ATTENTION, PLEASE? I HAVE AN ANNOUNCEMENT TO MAKE TO THE WHOLE STAFF...

AS YOU KNOW, THE COUNTRY IS NOW ENDURING A COMPLETE BREAKDOWN OF CONFIDENCE IN OUR LENDING INSTITUTIONS. AS A MEMBER OF THE BANKING COMMITTEE, I HAVE HAD A FRONT ROW SEAT THROUGHOUT THE CRISIS...

I DON'T BELIEVE IT... SHE'S GOING TO DO IT!
SHE'S READY! SHE'S MAKING HER MOVE!
MY VOTES ARE A MATTER OF PUBLIC RECORD...
HOT DAMN!

SHE'S RUNNING FOR **PRESIDENT!**
DAVENPORT IN '92!
THEREFORE, I HAVE DECIDED TO RESIGN.
WHITE HOUSE, HERE WE **COME!**

YES, I'VE DECIDED TO RESIGN — AS A MATTER OF HONOR OVER MY SMALL BUT DECISIVE ROLE IN BRINGING ON THE S&L CRISIS!
WHAT?

AS A RANKING MEMBER OF THE BANKING COMMITTEE, I SHOULD HAVE KNOWN BETTER. I SHOULD HAVE SEEN THAT DEREGULATION WOULD TURN OUR BANKS INTO CASINOS. FOR MY CARELESSNESS — AND THE CRISIS THAT RESULTED — I MUST ACCEPT FULL RESPONSIBILITY!

NOW, I KNOW WHAT YOU'RE ALL THINKING...
I THINK I JUST LOST MY JOB.
I DON'T BELIEVE THIS!
GREAT. WE'RE BEING CANNED.

YOU'RE THINKING, "POOR LACEY..."
I WONDER IF I CAN GET JOANIE'S JOB...
I'LL BE OKAY. THE OTHERS ARE DEAD MEAT!
I BETTER GET A RESUMÉ OUT...

BOSS? CAN I COME IN?
THERE'S NO USE TRYING TO CHANGE MY MIND, DEAR...

BUT LACEY...
I'LL BE RESIGNING ON THE HOUSE FLOOR THIS AFTERNOON. I HAVE TO OWN UP TO MY ROLE IN PRECIPITATING OUR CURRENT FISCAL CRISIS...

LACEY, **EVERYONE** MAKES MISTAKES. EVEN **GOOD** LEGISLATORS. YOU CAN'T JUST RESIGN OVER IT!
WHY NOT? WHY **CAN'T** I RESIGN OVER A **MATTER OF PRINCIPLE AND HONOR?**

I DON'T KNOW... IT'S JUST SO... SO JAPANESE!
GOOD DAY, DEAR.

MR. SPEAKER, DURING THE LAST EIGHT YEARS, THIS BODY HAS TAKEN A NUMBER OF ACTIONS THAT HAVE LED TO THE LARGEST FINANCIAL SCANDAL IN THE HISTORY OF THE WORLD.

THE S&L MESS HAS COVERED THIS INSTITUTION IN SHAME. AND YET NEVER HAVE SO MANY EXERTED THEMSELVES SO MIGHTILY TO AVOID TAKING PERSONAL RESPONSIBILITY FOR THE ROLES THEY PLAYED.

MY FRIENDS, I CANNOT JOIN YOU IN THAT EFFORT. TO ATONE FOR MY OWN ROLE IN THIS TRAGEDY, AND TO HELP RESTORE THE HONOR OF THIS HOUSE, I HAVE DECIDED TO RESIGN. THANK YOU VERY MUCH.

WHAT DO YOU THINK— MENOPAUSE?
AT 83? NO, THIS IS TROUBLE...

MS. CAUCUS! A WORD, IF YOU PLEASE!
YES, CONGRESSMAN?

WHAT'S WITH YOUR BOSS? WHAT'S THIS REALLY ABOUT?
LIKE SHE SAID, CONGRESSMAN, IT'S ABOUT HONOR...

IT'S ABOUT TAKING PERSONAL RESPONSIBILITY FOR ONE'S ACTIONS. IT'S ABOUT DOING THE RIGHT THING.

UH-HUH. HEY, IT'S NOT CANCER, IS IT?
NO, BUT YOU'RE SWEET TO BE CONCERNED.

GOOD EVENING. THE UNEXPECTED RESIGNATION OF A BELOVED CONGRESSWOMAN HAS WASHINGTON ABUZZ TODAY. ROLAND HEDLEY HAS DETAILS.

PETER, THE MOOD HERE TODAY IS MUCH LIKE IT WAS YESTERDAY. A SIMPLE, BUT STATELY ACT OF PRINCIPLE HAS LEFT THIS TOWN BADLY SHAKEN...

ON CAPITOL HILL, MRS. DAVENPORT'S STUNNED COLLEAGUES BEGAN TO REACT TO HER DRAMATIC DECISION TO STEP DOWN...

THE FEELING ON THE FLOOR IS IT MUST BE SOME SORT OF SEX SCANDAL.
OR CANCER. MY MONEY'S STILL ON CANCER.

PETER, I'M NOW TALKING TO MRS. JOAN CAUCUS, WHO WAS A KEY AIDE TO LACEY DAVENPORT. HAVE I GOT THAT RIGHT, MRS. CAUCUS?
UH... YES.

YOU'LL FORGIVE ME IF I'M NOT TOTALLY UP TO SPEED. I'M A SEASONED WAR CORRESPONDENT, AND I'VE BEEN PREOCCUPIED WITH EVENTS IN THE MID-EAST...
I SEE.

I'D BE THERE NOW, BUT IT WASN'T MY TURN IN THE ROTATION.
WELL, WE ALL HAVE OUR CROSSES TO BEAR. LACEY'S WAS HER SENSE OF COMPLICITY, OF RESPONSIBILITY...

I ONCE SAW A GUY GET BLOWN TO BITS.
SHOULD WE RESCHEDULE THIS?
GB Trudeau

MRS. CAUCUS, YOU WERE ONE OF MRS. DAVENPORT'S CLOSEST AIDES. HOW DO YOU FEEL SUDDENLY BEING OUT IN THE COLD?

WELL, I'M A WORKING MOTHER, SO OBVIOUSLY I'M NOT THRILLED. BUT THE CIRCUMSTANCES WERE BOTH COMPELLING AND UNIQUE.

I MEAN, I LOST MY JOB BECAUSE MY BOSS HAD THE COURAGE TO ACT ON HER REMARKABLE SENSE OF HONOR. I CAN LIVE WITH THAT.

BUT WON'T YOU BE TAINTED?
I CAN ONLY HOPE SO.
GB Trudeau

PETER, THE HEROINE OF CAPITOL HILL HAS JUST EMERGED. LET ME SEE IF I CAN GET A WORD WITH HER!

MRS. DAVENPORT, DO YOU THINK YOUR ACT OF CONSCIENCE WILL STRIKE A CHORD WITH...
I'M SORRY, BUT I DON'T DO TELE-VISION.

YOU DON'T DO **TELE-VISION?** HEE, HEE! CONGRESSWOMAN, **EVERYBODY** DOES TEL...
GET AWAY FROM ME, YOU DREARY LITTLE MAN!

HEROINE OR EMBITTERED MADWOMAN? YOU BE THE JUDGE, PETER!
NO, YOU BE, ROLAND.
©B Trudeau

IS THAT YOU, EVENING NEWS STAR?
WHAT A DISASTER. THEY SHOT MY BAD SIDE.

FIRST THING I NOTICED. BUT AT LEAST YOU'RE NOT GETTING YOUR HOUSE STAKED OUT.
OH, NO... LOOK AT THEM ON LACEY'S LAWN!

WHY DON'T THEY GIVE HER A BREAK? WHAT LOW-LIFE!
NOW, NOW, THOSE ARE MY BROTHERS IN JOURNALISM YOU'RE TALK-ING ABOUT!

PETER, ABC NEWS HAS JUST LEARNED THAT DAVENPORT IS BEHIND IN HER SEARS PAYMENTS!
KEEP DIGGING, ROLAND.
©B Trudeau

OKAY, KIDS, THAT'S IT— LIGHTS OUT!
AW, UNCLE BUTTSY! ONE MORE STORY ABOUT THE OLD DAYS! **PUL-LEEZE!**

WELL... OKAY, BUT THIS IS THE **LAST** ONE! ONCE UPON A TIME, WAY BACK IN 1934, THE AMERICAN TOBACCO COMPANY SET OUT TO SELL LUCKY STRIKES TO WOMEN, WHO HAD ONLY RECENTLY STARTED SMOKING IN LARGE NUMBERS...

MARKET RESEARCH REVEALED THAT WOMEN DISLIKED THE BRAND BECAUSE THE PACKAGE, WHICH USED TO BE GREEN, CLASHED WITH THEIR CLOTHES! THE SOLUTION? POPULARIZE GREEN AS THE FASHION COLOR OF CHOICE!
WOW.., HOW?

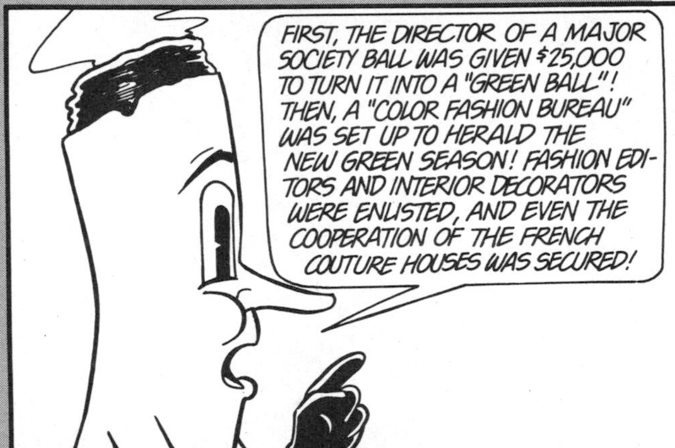
FIRST, THE DIRECTOR OF A MAJOR SOCIETY BALL WAS GIVEN $25,000 TO TURN IT INTO A "GREEN BALL"! THEN, A "COLOR FASHION BUREAU" WAS SET UP TO HERALD THE NEW GREEN SEASON! FASHION EDITORS AND INTERIOR DECORATORS WERE ENLISTED, AND EVEN THE COOPERATION OF THE FRENCH COUTURE HOUSES WAS SECURED!

BEFORE LONG, GREEN WAS **THE** COLOR OF AMERICAN FASHION! HORDES OF WOMEN STARTED BUYING AND SMOKING LUCKY STRIKES AS AN **ACCESSORY!**
AND? AND?

...AND THEY ALL DIED HAPPILY EVER AFTER! **THOUSANDS** OF 'EM!
YEAAA! TELL IT **AGAIN!** TELL IT **AGAIN!**
GB Trudeau

ATTENTION THIEVES:

NO RADIO IN CAR!

HAVE YOU CONSIDERED GETTING A **JOB?** GETTING OFF DRUGS AND TAKING **CHARGE** OF YOUR LIFE? **THINK** ABOUT IT. HAVE A NICE DAY! ☺

ATTENTION NEIGHBORS:

RADIO IN CAR!

BIG SUCKER, TOO. A 600-WATT, EIGHT-SPEAKER PIONEER AM/FM, TAPE DECK, CD RACK SYSTEM. EAT YOUR **HEART** OUT!

ATTENTION STRANGERS:

RADIO IN CAR?

MAYBE THERE IS, MAYBE NOT. I AIN'T SAYING. WAY I FIGURE IT, IT AIN'T NONE OF YOUR DAMN BUSINESS.

DAY 26. FOR WHAT SEEMED LIKE AN ETERNITY, HE WAS HELD HOSTAGE TO HIS COMICALLY OBSESSIVE VACATION PLANS...

CALLED UP?
I REPORT IN THE MORNING.

I...I CAN'T BELIEVE IT!
WELL, IT WAS BOUND TO HAPPEN SOONER OR LATER...

BUT THERE'S OVER A **MILLION** RESERVISTS! WHY YOU?
PROBABLY BECAUSE I'M IN INTELLIGENCE. I SPEAK FLUENT VIETNAMESE.
GB Trudeau

OH. VIETNAM'S IN SAUDI ARABIA?
NO, IT'S LIKE THE NEXT COUNTRY OVER. NEAR FINLAND.

LIFE'S WEIRD, AIN'T IT? TONIGHT I'M IN MALIBU, AND IN 48 HOURS, I'LL BE SITTING IN A DESERT 12,000 MILES AWAY...
FZZT!

...BROILING IN A CHEMICAL WARFARE SUIT IN THE 120° HEAT! WHICH REMINDS ME, I BETTER GET MY HELMET REMOVED...

GB Trudeau

HOW'S THAT DONE?
THEY FREEZE IT AND CUT IT AWAY LIKE AN AVOCADO. STRICTLY OUTPATIENT.

B.D., IT'S SID.
I DON'T WANT TO TALK TO HIM. EVERYONE'S CALLING TO OFFER CONSOLATION—LIKE I ALREADY DIED!

COME ON, B.D.—ONCE YOU'RE OVER THERE, YOU'RE GONNA **MISS** ALL THE PEOPLE IN YOUR LIFE—EVEN SID!

YEAH... I GUESS YOU'RE RIGHT. GIMME THAT...
GB Trudeau

HELLO?
B.D.! I KNOW YOU'RE PRESSED, BABE, SO BOTTOM LINE—CAN I DATE HER? BE A PAL!

WELCOME ABOARD, SOLDIER.
OH... THANK YOU, SIR!

VIETNAM ERA?
YES, SIR. BUT I LIKE THIS MISSION A **WHOLE** LOT MORE! CLEAR GOALS, VIABLE STRATEGY, SUPPORT AT HOME!

YOU GOT A FAMILY?
NO, SIR. JUST A GIRLFRIEND. BUT I'VE NEVER BEEN AWAY FROM HER. SHE'S GOING TO BE PRETTY LOST WITHOUT ME.

WELL, OKAY, BUT JUST DINNER — I'M ENGAGED.

SO WHAT DO YOU DO IN CIVILIAN LIFE, SOLDIER?
I'M A TALENT MANAGER, COLONEL. HOW ABOUT YOURSELF, SIR?

I'M A FLORIST. IT'S BEEN **YEARS** SINCE ANYONE'S CALLED ME "SIR"...

I DON'T KNOW WHY THEY WANT ME. I'M A PRETTY SORRY EXCUSE FOR A SOLDIER. I'M OUT OF SHAPE, I'VE FORGOTTEN ALL THE DRILLS, I CAN'T LOAD AN M-16...

I CAN'T EVEN REMEMBER HOW TO USE THE F-WORD!
EASY. YOU JUST USE IT LIKE A COMMA.

THIS IS ROLAND HEDLEY, REPORTING FROM SOMEWHERE IN THE MIDEAST!

HERE AT AN UNDISCLOSED LOCATION, AN UNIDENTIFIED TRANSPORT PLANE DISGORGED A CLASSIFIED NUMBER OF COMBATANTS!

I'M SPEAKING WITH ONE OF THE NEW ARRIVALS, WHOSE NAME AND RANK AND NATIONAL IDENTITY WE CANNOT REVEAL AT THIS TIME...
UNITED

WHY THE HELL **NOT?**
HEY!
UM...OKAY, SO HE'S FROM AN ENGLISH-SPEAKING ARMY.

PETER, I'M SPEAKING TO TWO NEW ARRIVALS IN THE GULF TODAY — A RAW RECRUIT, AND A SEASONED RESERVIST! YOUR FIRST REACTIONS, GUYS!

WELL, IT'S A LITTLE WARM, BUT HEY, WE'RE HERE TO FIGHT FOR DEMOCRACY AND AGAINST TYRANNY, AND THAT'S WHAT WE'RE GONNA DO!

GIMME A BREAK! WE'RE HERE FOR CHEAP OIL! WE'RE HERE SO WE DON'T NEED AN ENERGY POLICY! WE'RE HERE SO BUSH CAN DRIVE A BOAT SO OVERPOWERED IT'S FAVORED BY DRUG SMUGGLERS!

THAT'S... THAT'S AWFUL!
DON'T THEY **BRIEF** YOU GUYS?
VIVA LA DIFFERENCE, PETER!
©B Trudeau

HEY, SOLDIER! MIND IF I JOIN YOU?

PRETTY GRIM RATIONS, EH? OF COURSE, THIS IS A FEAST COMPARED TO THE FARE I DINED ON DURING THE SEVEN-DAY WAR! WE HAD TO PICK THE SCORPIONS OUT OF OUR STEW!

NOT THAT A FEW SCORPIONS WOULDN'T HAVE TASTED PRETTY GOOD DURING THE CIVIL WAR IN ANGOLA! AH, WELL, NO ONE EVER SAID IT WAS EASY BEING A WAR CORRESPONDENT!

ESPECIALLY IF YOU LOOK LIKE A DUCK HUNTER.
UM... RIGHT. ANY IDEA WHERE I CAN GET ONE OF THOSE HELMETS?
©B Trudeau

ANYBODY HEARD ANYTHING ABOUT DEPLOYMENT YET?
NOPE.
THE LID'S BEEN ON FOR WEEKS.

MAN, THAT'S THE WORST PART—NEVER KNOWING WHAT'S GOING ON! I REMEMBER THAT FROM 'NAM!
USE A CIGARETTE, MAN?

YEAH... YEAH, I COULD. I HAVEN'T SMOKED IN YEARS, BUT MAYBE IT'LL SETTLE MY NERVES. THANKS, BUDDY!

AIN'T WAR A BITCH?
OH, I DUNNO...
©B Trudeau

'MORNING, SOLDIER!
WELL, IF IT ISN'T THE COMPANY FLORIST! YOU BEEN ASSIGNED YET, COLONEL?

NO. HAVE YOU?
NOPE. I'VE BEEN SITTING AROUND EVER SINCE WE ARRIVED...

THAT'S ANOTHER THING I REMEMBER FROM THE NAM— LOTS OF SITTING AROUND! YOU WANT TO KNOW WHAT THE REAL ENEMY IS HERE?...
GB Trudeau

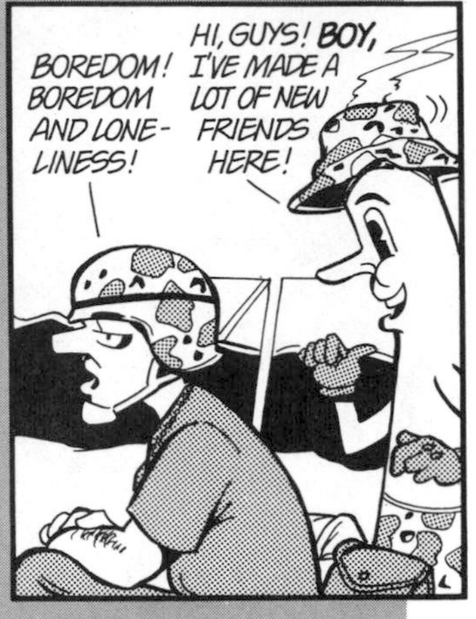
BOREDOM! BOREDOM AND LONELINESS!
HI, GUYS! BOY, I'VE MADE A LOT OF NEW FRIENDS HERE!

OKAY, GENTLEMEN, HERE'S THE IRRIGATION DRILL...
ONE

TO FEND OFF HEAT DISORDER, YOU GOTTA HYDRATE! SIX GALLONS A DAY—THAT'S 24 OF THESE BOTTLES!
WAT
32 FL. OZS
ER
OZS.

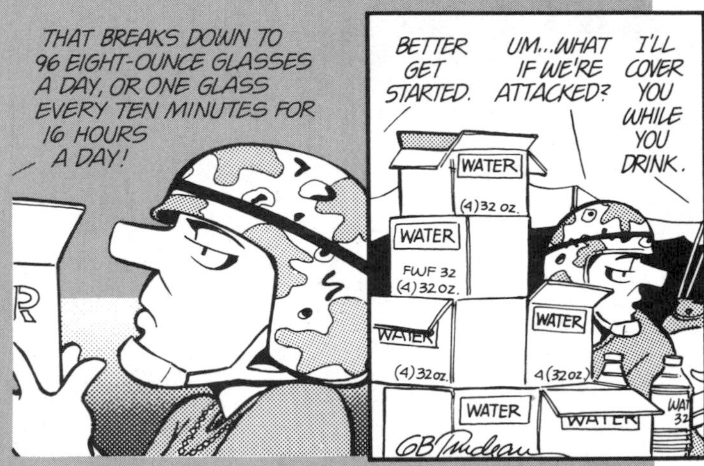
THAT BREAKS DOWN TO 96 EIGHT-OUNCE GLASSES A DAY, OR ONE GLASS EVERY TEN MINUTES FOR 16 HOURS A DAY!
BETTER GET STARTED.
UM...WHAT IF WE'RE ATTACKED?
I'LL COVER YOU WHILE YOU DRINK.
WATER
(4) 32 OZ.
WATER
FWF 32
(4) 32 OZ.
WATER
WATER
(4) 32 oz.
4 (32 oz.)
WATER
WATER
GB Trudeau

SIX GALLONS OF WATER A DAY? THAT CAN'T BE RIGHT...
THIS IS THE DESERT, CORPORAL!

WITHOUT CONSTANT WATER INFUSION, YOU'RE DEAD MEAT—YOU DEHYDRATE IN A BLINK! WATER IS EVERYTHING HERE, IT'S THE DIFFERENCE BETWEEN LIFE AND DEATH! GET IT, SOLDIER?
WATER

YES, SIR, I GET IT.
YOU GET IT, COLONEL?

OF COURSE I GET IT— I'M A FLORIST.
DAMN WEEKEND WARRIORS...
GB Trudeau

CORPORAL! GOT A MINUTE TO TALK TO US?
SORRY, MAN. I'M BEHIND IN MY WATER REGIMEN...

YOUR WATER REGIMEN? WHAT ARE YOU GUYS ON, ANYWAY?
SIX GALLONS A DAY.

SIX GALLONS? YOU'RE ISSUED **SIX** GALLONS EVERY DAY?
CORRECT.
THAT'S FUNNY— THE PRESS ONLY GETS ONE GALLON...
COULD BE A STORY THERE.

PETER, I'M SOMEWHERE IN THE MIDEAST, TALKING TO ARMY CAPTAIN ED LATOUR. CAPTAIN, WHAT LESSONS FROM THE GRENADA AND PANAMA INVASIONS HAVE YOU BEEN ABLE TO APPLY HERE?

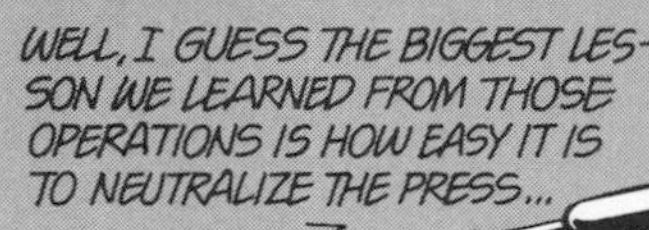
WELL, I GUESS THE BIGGEST LESSON WE LEARNED FROM THOSE OPERATIONS IS HOW EASY IT IS TO NEUTRALIZE THE PRESS...

WE FOUND THAT WE CAN CONTROL THE PRESS POOL, GIVE THEM BASICALLY SQUAT, AND THERE ISN'T A DAMN THING THEY CAN DO ABOUT IT!

UM... I SEE. ANY OTHER LESSONS?
YES, BUT THEY'RE CLASSIFIED.

...AND IF OUR BOYS **DO** GO ON THE OFFENSIVE, IT WILL BE THROUGH HARSH, UNFORGIVING DESERT TERRAIN LIKE THIS THAT THEY WILL HAVE TO ADVANCE!

FROM SOMEWHERE IN THE MIDEAST, THIS IS ROLAND HEDLEY!
ROLAND, WE UNDERSTAND THE NEED FOR SECURITY, BUT COULD YOU TELL US WHAT GENERAL AREA YOU'RE REPORTING FROM?

NO, PETER, I'M AFRAID I CAN'T GIVE YOU THAT INFORMATION.
C'MON, JUST THE REGION...

NO, REALLY, I'M LOST.
I SEE. WELL, GOOD LUCK, ROLAND!

BRAVO! LET'S GIVE A BIG HAND TO MISS SCHNAPPS! WASN'T SHE WONDERFUL, FOLKS? THANKS, KID!

OKAY! THAT BRINGS US TO OUR FINAL ACT! WARNING: THIS GUY IS OUTRAGEOUS!

IN HIS OWN COUNTRY, HE'S CONSIDERED TOO DANGER-OUS, TOO OUT THERE FOR T.V.! BUT HERE, HE'S A HERO! WE CAN'T GET ENOUGH OF HIM!

IF FOR SOME REASON YOU'RE STILL NOT HIP TO THIS GUY'S ACT, LEMME TELL YA, HE'S GONNA KILL YOU! HE'S GONNA PUT YOU AWAY!

SO LET'S GIVE A NICE, WARM SOVIET WEL-COME TO...

...MR. BUTTSKY!
OH, YEAH! THANK YOU FOR SMOKING! LEMME HEAR YA SAY "DA"!
DAAAA!

YO, CHECK IT OUT...
WHAT'S UP?

FIVE BUCKS ON THE SCORPION.
NO WAY. THAT SNAKE CAME TO KICK BUTT!

WAY TO GO, SNAKE! YOU BE THE BADDEST OF THE LOWLIFE!
HEY, SCORPION! YOU CALL THAT A FIGHT? YOU WEENIE!

THAT'LL BE FIVE BUCKS, MY MAN!
THE NAME'S B.D.—WHO ARE YOU?

RAYMOND. RAYMOND HIGHTOWER.
YOU LOOK FAMILIAR, MAN. DO I KNOW YOU FROM SOMEPLACE?

HI. MY NAME IS RAY HIGHTOWER, AND I JUST WANT TO SAY THE DESERT SUCKS!
FROM THE TUBE! I SAW YOU BEFORE I LEFT!

HOW LONG YOU BEEN IN THE GULF, RAY?
43 DAYS, MAN. AND I'LL TELL YOU ONE THING—I SURE DIDN'T BARGAIN FOR THIS CRAP WHEN I UPPED!

I WAS GONNA BE ALL I COULD BE, UNDERSTAND? I WAS GONNA GET A FREE EDUCATION, SEE THE WORLD, LEARN HOW TO PROGRAM COMPUTERS! IT WAS TODAY'S ARMY! NOBODY SAID ANYTHING ABOUT ACTUALLY HAVING TO FIGHT!

SIGH...

DAMN, I FEEL BETRAYED!
YEAH, T.V. ADS CAN TRIP YOU UP THAT WAY...

HEY, CHECK THIS OUT— JAY LENO'S COMING OVER HERE TO DO A U.S.O. THANKSGIVING SHOW!
TARS & STRIPES

GREAT. IS HE BRINGING ANYONE?
WELL, IT DOESN'T SAY HERE...

...BUT YOU GOTTA FIGURE HE'LL BRING ALONG SOME **MAJOR** BABES, THE WAY BOB HOPE USED TO!
STARS AND STRIP

OF COURSE, YOU'LL HAVE TO WEAR A TURKEY COSTUME...
I'D BE **HONORED,** MR. LENO!

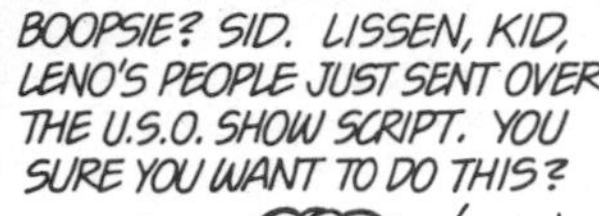

BOOPSIE? SID. LISSEN, KID, LENO'S PEOPLE JUST SENT OVER THE U.S.O. SHOW SCRIPT. YOU SURE YOU WANT TO DO THIS?

OF **COURSE** I'M SURE, SID! EVERYONE IN TOWN IS **DYING** TO GO TO THE GULF! IT'S A GREAT HONOR!
SLURP!

UH-HUH... HAVE YOU READ THE SCRIPT, BABE?
NO, BUT I'M SURE IT'S GREAT!

"HI! I'M YOUR LITTLE TURKEY! WHO WILL DRESS ME?"
YOU MEAN THERE'S AUDIENCE PARTICIPATION?

HI, KID! I WAS IN THE NEIGHBORHOOD AND THOUGHT I'D DROP OFF YOUR U.S.O. SCRIPT!
THANKS, SID! LOOK WHAT JUST ARRIVED— MY TURKEY COSTUME!

GOOD LUCK GETTING THAT THROUGH SAUDI CUSTOMS!
I STILL CAN'T BELIEVE I WAS ASKED! **TOUT** HOLLYWOOD WANTS TO GO!

ESPECIALLY 40-SOMETHING ENTERTAINERS STILL WORKING ON THEIR VIETNAM GUILT.
WELL, THAT'S NOT WHY **I'M** GOING! I'M GOING TO PERFORM FOR 100,000 CUTE GUYS IN COOL UNIFORMS!

ONE OF WHOM IS YOUR BOYFRIEND.
OH... RIGHT. I BETTER ADD A FEW FEATHERS.

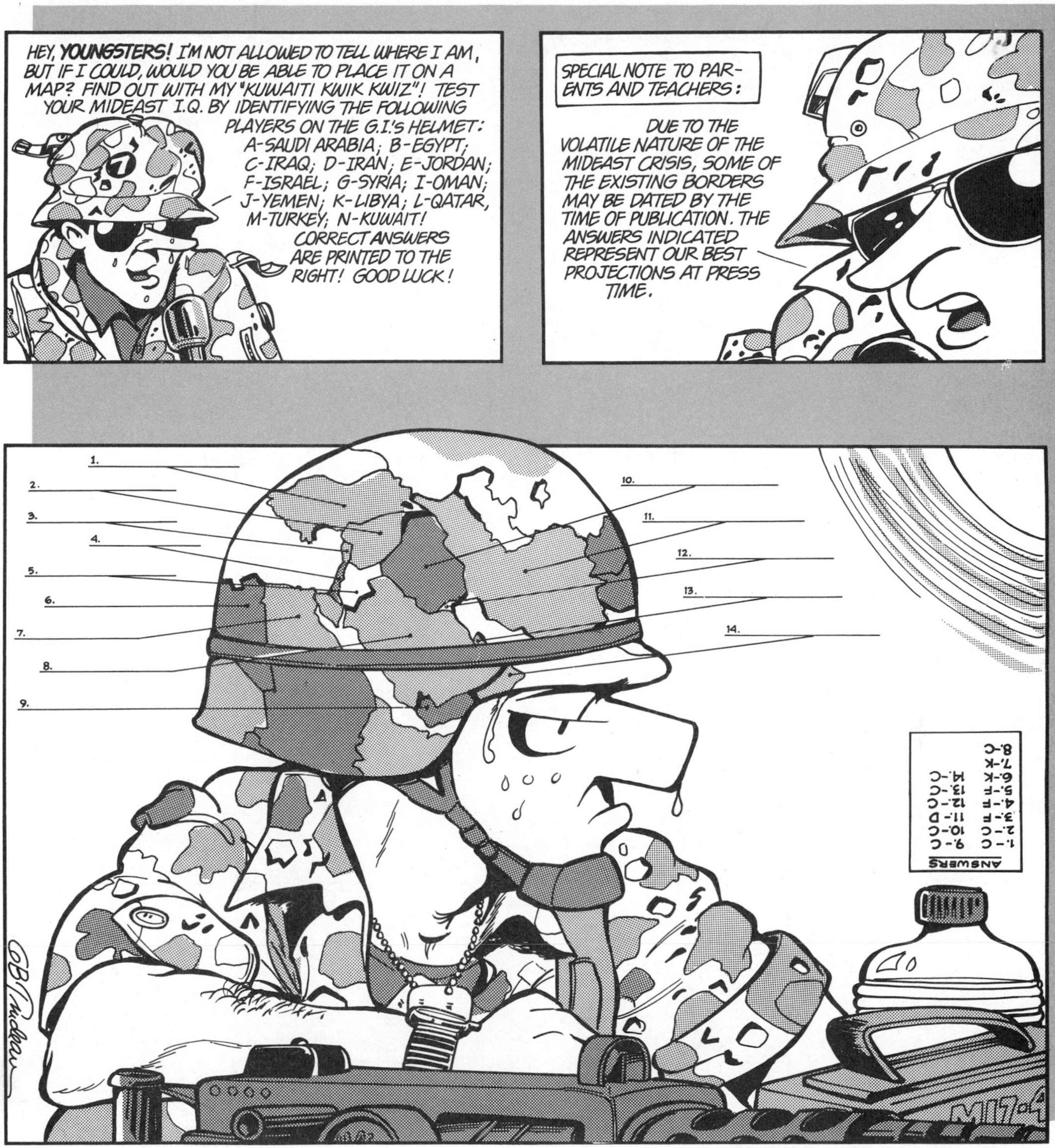

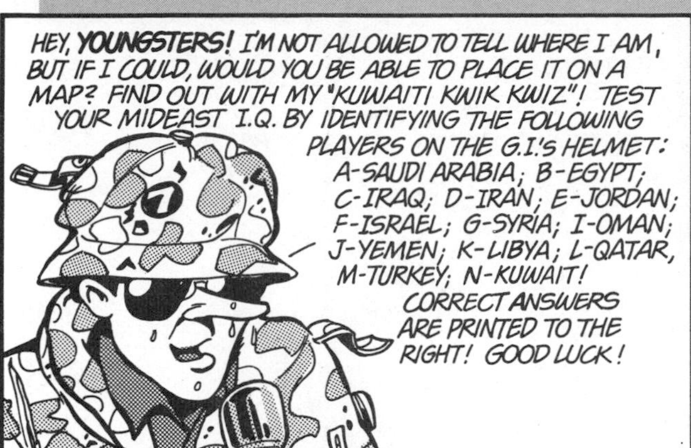

1. ______
2. ______
3. ______
4. ______
5. ______
6. ______
7. ______
8. ______
9. ______
10. ______
11. ______
12. ______
13. ______
14. ______

ANSWERS

1.-C 9.-C
2.-C 10.-C
3.-F 11.-D
4.-F 12.-C
5.-F 13.-C
6.-K 14.-C
7.-K
8.-C

M17-4

$33 A BARREL AND **RISING!** AND WITH NO INCREASE IN OUR FIXED COSTS! UNIVERSAL PETROLEUM IS **BACK**!

'COURSE, WE'VE GOT A LITTLE P.R. PROBLEM. THERE'S A LOT OF PUBLIC RESENTMENT OVER THE DAILY HIKES AT THE GAS PUMPS...

WE THINK THE ANSWER IS AN APPEAL TO PEOPLE'S PATRIOTISM—TO MAKE THEM FEEL **GOOD** ABOUT BEING GOUGED! YOU HAVE ANY QUALMS ABOUT THIS KIND OF APPROACH?

NO... NO, I USED TO, BUT THAT WAS LONG AGO...
GOOD. I LIKE YOU, KID.
GB Trudeau

YOU'VE GOT THAT LOOK AGAIN, MIKE.
THEY GAVE ME AN OIL ACCOUNT TODAY—UNIVERSAL PETROLEUM.

THEY WANT A CAMPAIGN TO BLUNT CONSUMER RESENTMENT OVER HIGH PRICES. THEY'RE WORRIED PEOPLE MIGHT ACTUALLY START THINKING ABOUT ALTERNATIVE ENERGY SOURCES.

THE IDEA IS TO PITCH OIL AS A VIRILE, PATRIOTIC ENERGY SOURCE, AS OPPOSED TO SOLAR AND ALCOHOL, WHICH ARE WIMPY, TREE-HUGGING FUELS...
WHAT'S THE CAMPAIGN CALLED?

"OIL: REAL FUEL FOR REAL CARS."
THIS WOULDN'T BE GEARED TOWARDS MEN, WOULD IT?
GB Trudeau

OH, BY THE WAY, KID, I GOT YOU A MEET ON A BIG NEW AD CAMPAIGN—UNIVERSAL PETROLEUM!

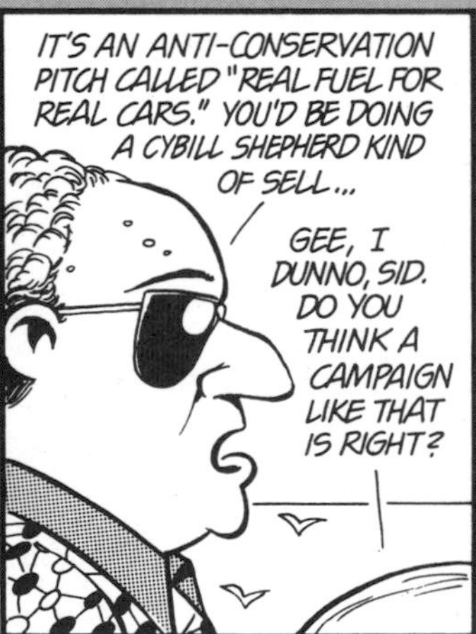
IT'S AN ANTI-CONSERVATION PITCH CALLED "REAL FUEL FOR REAL CARS." YOU'D BE DOING A CYBILL SHEPHERD KIND OF SELL...
GEE, I DUNNO, SID. DO YOU THINK A CAMPAIGN LIKE THAT IS RIGHT?

HEE, HEE...

YOU AND TOTO STILL MISS KANSAS, DON'T YOU, KID?
I JUST WISH B.D. WERE HERE. HE USED TO HANDLE ALL OUR ETHICS.
GB Trudeau

AN AD FOR UNIVERSAL PETROLEUM? I DUNNO, SID, I'M NOT SO SURE THAT THAT'S A GOOD CAREER MOVE FOR ME...

LOOK, KID, AT LEAST MEET WITH THE CREATIVE DIRECTOR. HE'S FLYING OUT HERE TODAY. AND HE SAYS YOU KNOW HIM — MIKE DOONESBURY?

MIKE? NO. THERE MUST BE SOME MISUNDERSTANDING! MIKE WOULD **NEVER** COMPROMISE HIMSELF TO FLACK FOR AN OIL COMPANY!

DOONESBURY, M. I'M BOOKED STRAIGHT THROUGH TO HELL.
I'LL CHECK.
TWA

IT'S BEEN TOO LONG, KIDDO...
OH, MIKEY, I'M SO EXCITED ABOUT DOING THE AD!

YOU ARE? REALLY?
OF COURSE! I MEAN, THE WHOLE THING IS JUST SO KARMIC...

I ALWAYS KNEW THAT ONE DAY YOU AND I WOULD WORK ON A CREATIVE PROJECT TOGETHER! AND NOW HERE WE ARE — ABOUT TO COLLABORATE ON A **MAJOR** T.V. AD!
IT'S JUST TOO BAD THE CLIENT'S A PIG.
WELL, I THINK WE SHOULD TALK ABOUT THAT...

YOU KNOW, MIKE, WHEN SID FIRST TOLD ME ABOUT THE OIL AD, I THOUGHT, LIKE, FORGET IT, THOSE GUYS ARE BAD NEWS!

BUT THEN I THOUGHT, WHOA, HOLD MY HORSES! IF **MIKE** — WHO HAS MORE MORALS THAN ANYONE I KNOW — IF **HE'S** INVOLVED WITH THE PROJECT, THEN IT **MUST** BE OKAY, RIGHT?

RIGHT?

BOOPSIE, LET'S TAKE A WALK.
WALK? YOU SILLY, NOBODY WALKS IN L.A.!

LOOK, BOOPSIE, I DON'T ENJOY WORKING FOR CLIENTS LIKE UNIVERSAL PETROLEUM ANY MORE THAN YOU DO, BUT I HAVE TO LIVE IN THE REAL WORLD...

IF YOU LOOK HARD ENOUGH, **ALL** COMPANIES ARE PROBABLY DOING **SOMETHING** OBJECTIONABLE. ALSO, I'VE GOT A FAMILY NOW. LIKE IT OR NOT, THAT CHANGES EVERYTHING...

I KNOW, MIKE, I UNDERSTAND...
DO YOU?

MIKE, I **DID** HAVE NINE CHILDREN DURING THE 13TH CENTURY.
OH... RIGHT. HOW'RE THEY ALL MAKING OUT?
©B Trudeau

THE POINT IS, BOOPSIE, YOU CAN'T BE TOO QUICK TO JUDGE! OUT OF FAIRNESS, YOU HAVE TO CONSIDER THE CLIENT'S PERSPECTIVE AS SCRUPULOUSLY AS YOUR OWN.

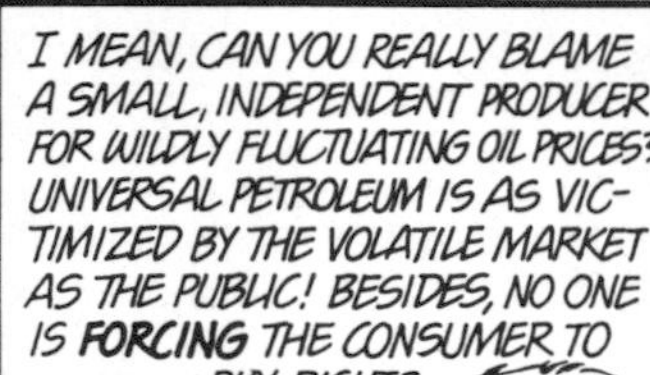

I MEAN, CAN YOU REALLY BLAME A SMALL, INDEPENDENT PRODUCER FOR WILDLY FLUCTUATING OIL PRICES? UNIVERSAL PETROLEUM IS AS VICTIMIZED BY THE VOLATILE MARKET AS THE PUBLIC! BESIDES, NO ONE IS **FORCING** THE CONSUMER TO BUY, RIGHT?

I SUPPOSE SO. YOU KNOW, IT'S FUNNY, MIKE...
WHAT IS?

I NEVER NOTICED THAT YOUR EYE TWITCHED BEFORE.
UM... IT'S THE AIR POLLUTION OUT HERE. WICKED.
©B Trudeau

BOOPSIE! OVER HERE! COME MEET OUR CLIENT, MR. ANDREWS!

OH, MR. ANDREWS, WHAT A PLEASURE! I'VE ALWAYS ADMIRED YOUR... UM...PETROLEUM PRODUCTS! IN FACT, MY BOYFRIEND IS OVER FIGHTING FOR THEM RIGHT NOW!
IS THAT RIGHT?

YUP! HERE'S A NEW PICTURE OF HIM IN HIS DESERT FATIGUES...
WHOA! HOLD THE PHONE! NOW, **THAT'S** EXPLOITABLE!

EXPLOITABLE?
IT'S JUST A TECHNICAL TERM.
I WANT A 20-FOOT BLOW-UP BEHIND HER!
©B Trudeau

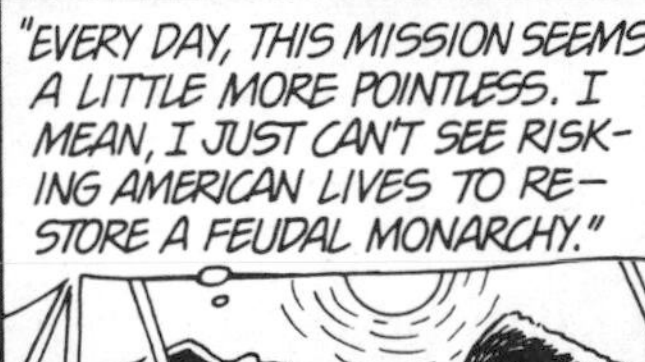

"IF THERE'S ANY LESSON IN ALL OF THIS, IT'S THAT OUR COUNTRY'S GOING TO HAVE TO FINALLY GET SERIOUS ABOUT ITS OIL HABIT..."

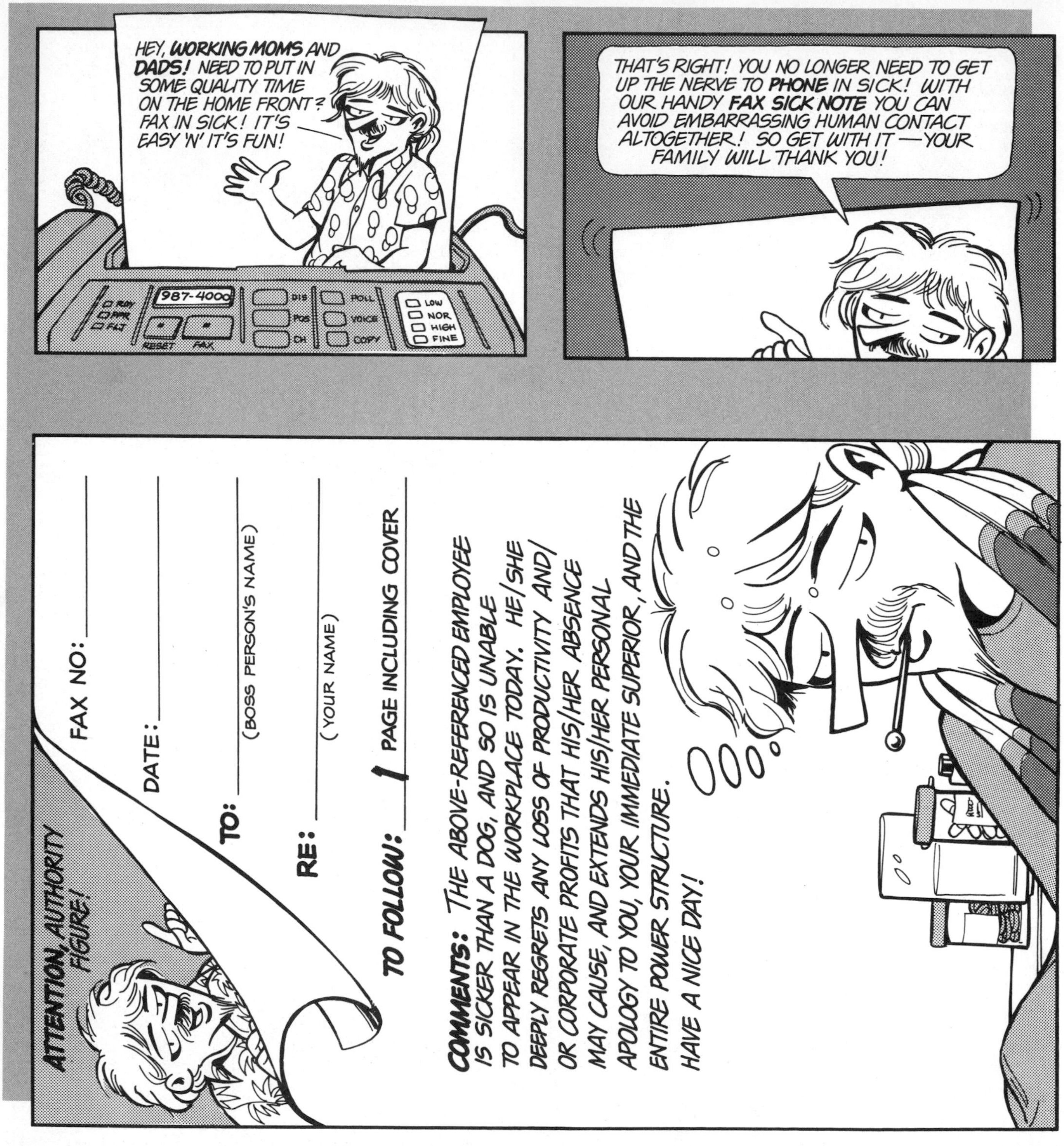

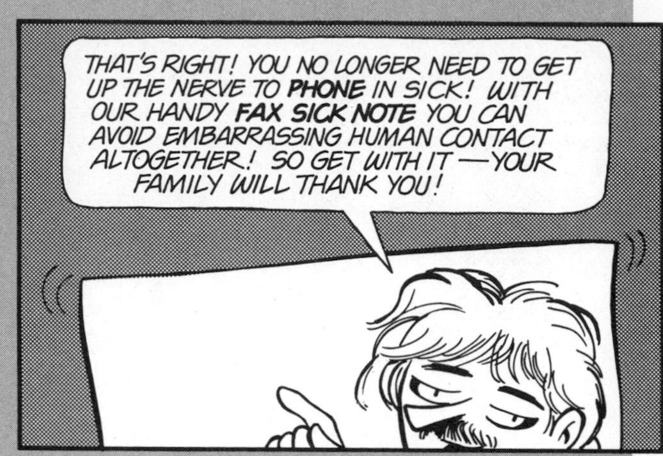

ATTENTION, AUTHORITY FIGURE!

FAX NO: ____

DATE: ____

TO: ____ (BOSS PERSON'S NAME)

RE: ____ (YOUR NAME)

TO FOLLOW: 1 PAGE INCLUDING COVER

COMMENTS: THE ABOVE-REFERENCED EMPLOYEE IS SICKER THAN A DOG, AND SO IS UNABLE TO APPEAR IN THE WORKPLACE TODAY. HE/SHE DEEPLY REGRETS ANY LOSS OF PRODUCTIVITY AND/OR CORPORATE PROFITS THAT HIS/HER ABSENCE MAY CAUSE, AND EXTENDS HIS/HER PERSONAL APOLOGY TO YOU, YOUR IMMEDIATE SUPERIOR, AND THE ENTIRE POWER STRUCTURE.

HAVE A NICE DAY!

HI, I'M PETER NEVILLE FROM SEATTLE, WASHINGTON, AND I'D LIKE TO ASK OUR JAPANESE AND GERMAN FRIENDS TO GET A LITTLE MORE SERIOUS ABOUT BURDEN-SHARING.

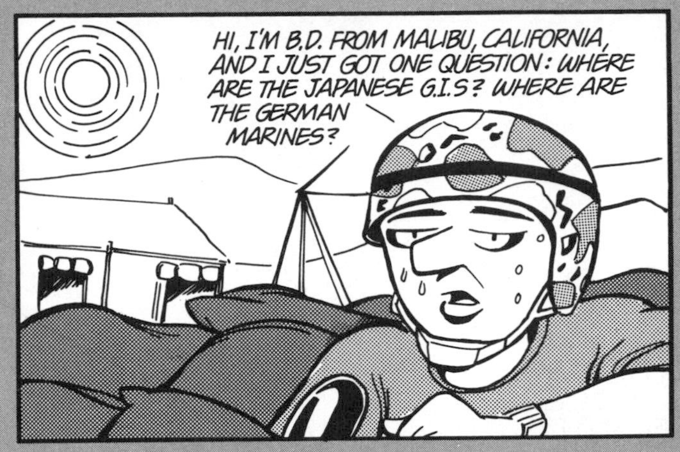
HI, I'M B.D. FROM MALIBU, CALIFORNIA, AND I JUST GOT ONE QUESTION: WHERE ARE THE JAPANESE G.I.S? WHERE ARE THE GERMAN MARINES?

I'M JORGE CAPITO FROM CORPUS CHRISTI, TEXAS, AND I WANT TO KNOW WHY THE CHIEF BENEFICIARIES OF THIS ACTION AREN'T PUTTIN' THEIR BUTTS ON THE LINE LIKE WE ARE!

HI, I'M JEAN FOUCHET FROM NEW ORLEANS, AND I JUST WANT TO SAY TO THE GERMANS AND JAPANESE THAT AFTER HAVING TO DEFEND OURSELVES FROM **YOU** DURING WWII, IT'S AN **OBSCENITY** THAT WE'RE NOW OUT HERE DEFENDING **YOUR** OIL INTERESTS!

HI, I'M LOU BIRD FROM TULSA, OKLAHOMA! HONEY, SELL THE HONDA!

SIR, WE'RE SENSING SOME RESENTMENT ON THE FRONT LINES...
THAT WON'T SHOW UP IN THE POLLS, WILL IT?
GB Trudeau

ADIOS, MR. SUN!
ON HIS WAY TO THE GULF...

YOU KNOW, IT'S ODD, MIKE. B.D. AND HIS BUDDIES ARE OVER 12,000 MILES AWAY, BUT I CAN FEEL THEIR VIBRATIONS AS STRONGLY AS IF THEY WERE COMING FROM BURBANK!

I SENSE A DEEP LONGING IN THEIR DREAMS, MIKE — A COLLECTIVE CRY FROM THE HEART!
©B Trudeau

BEER... BEER... BEER...

YO, B.D.?... B.D.? YOU AWAKE?
I AM NOW.

IT'S DARK, MAN. I'VE NEVER SEEN IT SO DARK!
NEW MOON. TRADITIONALLY, THE BEST TIME TO LAUNCH AN OFFENSIVE OPERATION.

AND NOW I'M SUPPOSED TO SLEEP?
YOU BROUGHT IT UP, RAY...
©B Trudeau

WHERE YOU FROM ORIGINALLY, MAN?
HUH?... WHAT?

WHERE YOU FROM? WHAT TOWN?
SMALL TOWN IN OHIO. YOU NEVER HEARD OF IT.

I KNEW YOU WEREN'T FROM A BIG CITY. YOU CAN ALWAYS TELL THE BIG-CITY BOYS. SOMETHING IN THE WAY THEY WALK...
THAT RIGHT?

ALSO, THEY ALL GOT "NO RADIO" SIGNS ON THEIR TENTS.
YOU KNOW, I WAS WONDERING ABOUT THAT...
©B Trudeau

YOU KNOW HOW I ENDED UP IN THE SERVICE, MAN? MY WIFE! SHE TALKED ME INTO IT...
IS THAT RIGHT?

I'D JUST BEEN LAID OFF, AND I WAS GOING NOWHERE REAL FAST, SO MY WIFE SENT AWAY FOR THESE ARMY BROCHURES AND STARTED READING THEM TO ME OVER BREAKFAST...

SO, SUDDENLY I'M THINKING, COOL, I'LL ENLIST. I'LL LEARN COMPUTERS, I'LL GET MONEY FOR COLLEGE, RIGHT? RIGHT?
UH HUH...

YO, I'M NOT BORING YOU, AM I, MAN?
OF COURSE NOT, RAY. AT 0400, I CAN'T GET ENOUGH OF YOUR LIFE STORY.
GB Trudeau

SO ANYWAY, THEY TOLD ME I'D GET COMPUTER TRAINING – AND I FELL FOR IT! HELL, I HAVEN'T EVEN **SEEN** A COMPUTER SINCE I ENLISTED!
YOU'RE NOT MISSING MUCH...

YOU KNOW HOW TO USE A COMPUTER? HEY, CAN YOU TEACH ME HOW, MAN?
> SIGH...< SURE, RAY, SURE, I CAN TEACH YOU...

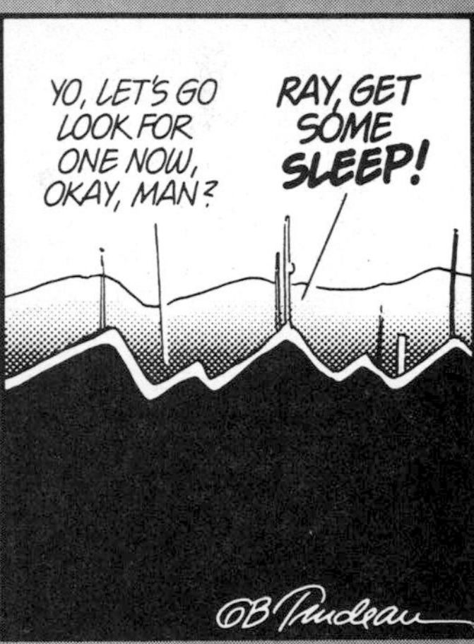
YO, LET'S GO LOOK FOR ONE NOW, OKAY, MAN?
RAY, GET SOME SLEEP!
GB Trudeau

SO I GET THIS "TO ANY SERVICE-PERSON" LETTER, SEE? AND IT'S VERY IM-PERSONAL...
HEY! RAY! GIVE THE CHATTER A **REST,** WILLYA? THE REST OF US NEED SOME DAMN **SLEEP,** OKAY?

HEY, COOL, MAN... IF THAT'S THE WAY YOU FEEL ABOUT IT...
THAT'S THE WAY I FEEL ABOUT IT! GOOD **NIGHT**!

GB Trudeau

YO, TURNS OUT IT WAS FROM PUB-LISHERS CLEARING HOUSE...
RAY!
OKAY, YOU MUGS, UP AND AT 'EM!

HI, FOLKS! EVER WONDER HOW YOUR COMMUNITY STANDARDS STACK UP AGAINST CINCINNATI'S?

DON'T YOU WISH YOU COULD MAKE UP YOUR OWN MIND ABOUT THE CONTROVERSIAL MAPPLETHORPE PHOTOS WITHOUT THE EMBARRASS-MENT OF ACTUALLY GO-ING TO SEE THEM?

WELL, NOW YOU CAN! IN COOPERATION WITH THIS NEWSPAPER, WE ARE DELIGHTED TO REPRODUCE FIVE OF THE PHOTOS THAT HAVE SO TESTED OUR COM-MITMENT TO FREEDOM OF EXPRESSION! ENJOY!

WELL, THAT'S IT! LET YOUR EDITOR KNOW WHAT YOU THINK! 'BYE FOR NOW!

WE'RE BACK. SUBJECT: PHILIP MORRIS DONATES 2 MILLION CIGARETTES TO THE DESERT SHIELD ARMED FORCES! GUEST: SLACKMEYER, SR., INDUSTRY APOLOGIST!

OKAY, DAD, WHAT GIVES HERE? WHY SEND SMOKES TO THE TROOPS?
THEY ASKED FOR 'EM! IN SOME OF THE MOST MOVING LETTERS I'VE EVER SEEN!

IT WAS A HUMANITARIAN GESTURE. I CATEGORICALLY REJECT YOUR SNIDE IMPLICATION THAT THE INDUSTRY IS TRYING TO HOOK YET ANOTHER GENERATION OF SOLDIERS!

HEY... MORE FREE SMOKES! I WONDER WHERE THEY CAME FROM...
WHO CARES? ENJOY!

HEY, BUDDY? YOU KNOW ANYTHING ABOUT THE SMOKES I KEEP FINDING ON MY BED?
HEE, HEE! YOU CAUGHT ME! I'M THE ONE WHO'S BEEN LEAVIN' 'EM FOR YOU!

AND WHO ARE YOU?
YOU CAN CALL ME "BUTTSY"! I'M THE BATTALION TOBACCO LIAISON!

ON BEHALF OF A GRATEFUL INDUSTRY, I'VE BEEN CHARGED WITH DISTRIBUTING 10,000 CARTONS OF CIGARETTES TO OUR FIGHTING MEN AND WOMEN — FREE OF CHARGE!

NO KIDDING? WHY?
OUT OF THE GOODNESS OF... WHOA! YOU KNOW YOU LOOK LIKE BOGART, RIGHT? PEOPLE TELL YOU THAT?

HEY, BUTTSY, HOW COULD YOU GET FREE SMOKES INTO HERE? THE PENTAGON'S GOT REGULATIONS AGAINST IT!
HOW COULD WE? HOW COULD WE NOT? LOOK AT THESE!

WHAT ARE THEY?
LETTERS! FROM BRAVE SERVICEMEN AND SERVICEGALS HERE IN THE GULF!

"DEAR PHILIP MORRIS: HELP! WE CAN'T GET SMOKES ON THE FRONT LINES! IF WE DON'T GET A SHIPMENT SOON, WE MIGHT ALL BECOME... BECOME..."
"NON-SMOKERS!"

"SIGNED, DESPERATE, SOMEWHERE IN THE MIDEAST."
WE HAVEN'T RECEIVED MAIL THAT MOVING SINCE THE CIVIL WAR!

WHERE YOU BEEN GETTIN' ALL THE SMOKES, MAN?
FROM BUTTSY.

WHO'S THAT?
TALL, SKINNY GUY OVER THERE. HE'S THE BATTALION'S TOBACCO LIAISON...

HE'S DISTRIBUTING 2 MILLION FREE SMOKES COURTESY OF PHILIP MORRIS... AS WELL AS FREE COUNSELING.
GB Trudeau

SEE, YOU CAN ALWAYS GIVE IT UP WHEN YOU GET **HOME!**
WOW... YOU SURE THERE ISN'T A CATCH?

HOW ABOUT YOU, GOOD BUDDY? CARE FOR SOME **FREE SMOKES?**
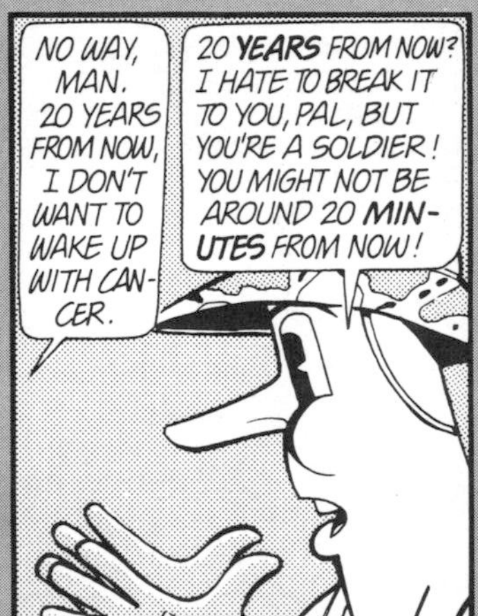
NO WAY, MAN. 20 YEARS FROM NOW, I DON'T WANT TO WAKE UP WITH CANCER.
20 **YEARS** FROM NOW? I HATE TO BREAK IT TO YOU, PAL, BUT YOU'RE A SOLDIER! YOU MIGHT NOT BE AROUND 20 **MINUTES** FROM NOW!

GB Trudeau

GOOD POINT.
THANK YOU. THIS **IS** MY SIXTH WAR.

HOW ABOUT YOU, SOLDIER? INTEREST YOU IN SOME FREE SMOKES?
NAH, MAN! I DON'T SMOKE...

REALLY? I'LL BET YOU JUST HAVEN'T TRIED THE RIGHT **BRAND!** MAY I SUGGEST **MARLBOROS**, THE CHOICE OF SO MANY SERVICE-PEOPLE! MARLBORO PROJECTS THE VALUES OF THE OLD WEST!

THE MARLBORO MAN IS RUGGED, INDEPENDENT, A COWBOY WHO DOESN'T RUN WITH THE HERD!
I DUNNO, MAN, I AIN'T NO COWBOY...
GB Trudeau

OKAY, THEN, MAYBE YOU'RE A **SOPHISTICATE!** A BENSON 'N' HEDGES SORT OF FELLOW!
HEY, YO, DAT'S **ME!**

YO, CHECK THIS OUT...

MY WIFE SENT ME THE NEW SWIMSUIT CALENDAR! ROLLED UP INSIDE A FLASHLIGHT! MAN, IS THAT LADY SECURE?

AND LOOK AT THIS— A WALKMAN WITH AN AIR-TIGHT WAIST PACK— TO KEEP THE SAND OUT!

AND TAPES OF ALL THE WORLD SERIES GAMES! MAN, DOES THIS WOMAN HAVE HER STUFF TOGETHER, OR WHAT?

UM... YEAH, SHE SURE SEEMS TO...
WHAT'D BOOPSIE SEND YOU?

UM... LOTS OF COOL STUFF. SALAD DRESSING... POST-IT NOTES...
AWRIGHT! BOLTS OF RAW SILK TO TRADE WITH BEDOUIN NOMADS!
GB Trudeau

HI THERE, MRS. D! JUST WANTED TO STOP BY TO SAY WELCOME HOME!
WELL, AREN'T YOU SWEET, OFFICER McBRIDE!

I SUPPOSE BY NOW YOU KNOW HOW UPSET THE NEIGHBORHOOD WAS TO LEARN YOU'RE NOT RUNNING FOR CONGRESS AGAIN...

I JUST HOPE YOU WEREN'T TOO ALARMED BY THE SCENE OUTSIDE YOUR HOUSE LAST NIGHT.
SCENE? WHAT SCENE WAS THAT, DEAR?

UM... 20,000 PEOPLE HELD A CANDLELIGHT VIGIL.
GRACIOUS! THEY BEHAVED THEMSELVES, I HOPE!
GB Trudeau

EXCUSE ME, MAN, I'M FROM THE SANITATION DEPARTMENT...
HOW MAY I HELP YOU, YOUNG MAN?

DO YOU, LIKE, KNOW ANYTHING ABOUT THE GONZO MESS OUT FRONT?
YES, I'M AFRAID THERE WAS A VIGIL LAST NIGHT. I'M TOLD THERE WERE 20,000 PEOPLE.

OH, WOW... YOU HAD 20,000 PEOPLE WAITING OUTSIDE YOUR HOUSE?
I'M DREADFULLY SORRY.

HEY, YOU'RE NOT, LIKE, YOKO ONO ARE YOU, MAN?
NO, DEAR, ARE YOU?
GB Trudeau

HI, BOSS. GUESS WHOSE DISTRICT OFFICE IS A MOB SCENE.
I WAS AFRAID OF THAT. COME IN, DEAR.

TAKE A LOOK AT THIS, LACEY. A PETITION FROM 28,000 CONSTITUENTS ASKING YOU TO RUN FOR CONGRESS AGAIN...

OH, DEAR... DEAR... I'M NOT SURE I'M UP TO THIS...

UP TO RUNNING?
NO, NO, WRITING 28,000 THANK YOU NOTES.
GB Trudeau

YOU SHOULD HAVE SEEN THE DISTRICT OFFICE, BOSS! IT'S PACKED WITH YOUR FORMER CONSTITUENTS, SOME OF THEM REFUSING TO LEAVE UNTIL YOU AGREE TO RUN AGAIN!

OH, DEAR. THAT WON'T DO. I BETTER ENDORSE MY SUCCES-SOR'S CAN-DIDACY AT ONCE!
SUCCESSOR? LACEY, YOU DON'T HAVE A SUCCESSOR IN EITHER PARTY!

YOUR OLD PAL VENTURA ANNOUNCED, BUT HE WAS BURNED IN EFFIGY DURING THE LABOR DAY PARADE AND HAD TO WITHDRAW! I MEAN YOUR SUPPORTERS ARE FANATICAL!

THANK YOU, DEAR. YOU MAKE ME SOUND LIKE MUSSOLINI.
LACEY, THEY LOVE YOU! LET THEM VOTE FOR YOU!
GB Trudeau

YOU SEE, LACEY, THE PROBLEM IS THAT WHILE SOMEBODY MIGHT HAVE RUN AGAINST YOU, NO-BODY WANTS TO RUN AGAINST YOUR EX-AMPLE!
WELL, MAYBE IT'S ALL FOR THE BETTER, DEAR.

ALL FOR THE BETTER? LACEY, IF THERE'S NO CANDIDATE, COME JANUARY, THERE'S GOING TO BE ONE LESS MEMBER OF THE U.S. CONGRESS!

I SEE YOUR POINT.
IT'S THE LEAST CONGRESS CAN DO. WE'VE ALL BEHAVED SO DREADFULLY!
GB Trudeau

HELLO?
HI, LACEY, IT'S JOANIE. HAVE YOU GIVEN ANY MORE THOUGHT TO BEING A WRITE-IN CANDIDATE?

WELL, YES, I HAVE, DEAR.. I SUP-POSE IF THERE'S NO OTHER CANDIDATE, IT'D BE IRRESPONSIBLE TO RULE IT OUT...
AND IF ELECTED, YOU'LL SERVE?

YES, BUT WITH ONE PROVISO.
WHAT'S THAT?

I MIGHT HAVE TO RESIGN AGAIN. OVER TAXES.
FAIR ENOUGH!
GB Trudeau

AND IN CALIFORNIA, A REMARKABLE ELECTION DAY DEVELOPMENT...

LACEY DAVENPORT, THE REPUBLICAN CONGRESS-WOMAN WHO RESIGNED LAST SUMMER OVER THE S&L CRISIS, HAS BEEN SWEPT BACK INTO OFFICE IN A WRITE-IN CAMPAIGN...

BOTH UNANNOUNCED AND UNOPPOSED, MRS. DAVENPORT RECEIVED 138,000 VOTES, AN EXTRAORDINARY FEAT THAT HAS STUNNED THE LOCAL POLITICAL ESTABLISHMENT!

MY REACTION? TO WHAT, DEAR?
IN TIGHT! IN TIGHT! SHE'S STILL A VIRGIN!
7

IS IT TRUE, DEAR? I ACTUALLY WON?
WON? YOU HAVE OVER 138,000 WRITE-IN VOTES! AND STILL COUNTING!

YOU CAN'T BE SERIOUS! 138,000 PEOPLE WROTE MY NAME IN?
IT'S UNPRECEDENTED!

GRACIOUS...
©B Trudeau

HOW WAS THEIR PENMANSHIP?
WHO CARES! FOR PETE'S SAKE, LACEY, BREAK OUT THE SHERRY!

LA-CEY! LA-CEY! LA-CEY!
HEAVENS! WHAT A RUCKUS!

I DON'T KNOW HOW MANY TIMES IN OUR HISTORY A WRITE-IN CANDIDATE HAS BEEN SENT TO CONGRESS, BUT I'M JUST THRILLED BEYOND WORDS TO BE ONE OF THEM!

I MUST HAVE THE MOST LOYAL FRIENDS ON EARTH! DO YOU KNOW WHAT ALL OF YOU ARE? DO YOU?
©B Trudeau

PERFECT DEARS!
GRACIOUS... DID YOU TELL THEM, DEAR?

MAKE SURE THAT'S GOOD AND SECURE, OKAY?
EXCUSE ME, SOL-DIER?
A-31

YOU TALKING TO ME?
NOT YET, BUT I'D LIKE TO. I'M ROLAND HED-LEY, OF ABC NEWS...

I'M DOING A PIECE ON WHAT THE MEN **REALLY** THINK OF WOMEN IN THE ARMED SERVICES —NOT THE OFFICIAL VIEW I KEEP GETTING FROM OFFICERS, BUT WHAT YOU GRUNTS ARE SAYING NOW THAT YOU'VE SEEN CHICKS IN ACTION!

SORRY, MAN, CAN'T HELP YOU...
WHY'S THAT?

I'M A CHICK.
WHAT?

I'M ALSO A LIEUTENANT CHICK.
WELL, COULD YOU POINT OUT A GUY TO ME? I'M ON DEADLINE.
A-31
©B'Trudeau

THERE HE IS!
THUMPA! THUMPA! THUM

MAN, LOOK AT THAT! HE TRAVELS WITH THREE CHOPPERS!
WELL, HE IS RUNNING THE WHOLE SHOW.

I WONDER WHAT THE OLD MAN'S GOING TO HARANGUE US ABOUT TODAY...

HOLD YOUR FIRE, MEN!
LOW MORALE, I'M GUESSING.

GOOD MORNING, LADIES AND GENTLEMEN! I'M RUNNING LATE, SO LET ME CUT TO THE CHASE!

LATELY THERE'S BEEN A LOT OF LOOSE TALK ABOUT THERE BEING A MORALE PROBLEM AMONG THE FIGHTING FORCES OF OPERATION DESERT SHIELD!

WELL, I'M HERE TO TELL YOU THERE IS NO MORALE PROBLEM! REPEAT, THERE IS NO MORALE PROBLEM! ANY TALK ABOUT MORALE PROBLEMS IS PURE POPPYCOCK!

DIS-MISSED!
WE MUST JUST HAVE AN ATTITUDE PROBLEM.
YEAH.

WHAT IS IT, SOLDIER?
GENERAL, IF THERE'S A MORALE PROBLEM, IT'S MOSTLY BECAUSE A LOT OF US ARE STILL CONFUSED OVER WHAT OUR MISSION IS...

WELL, LET ME JUST CLEAR UP YOUR CONFUSION, BOY! OUR MILITARY MISSION HAS THREE BASIC GOALS! ONE, TO DEFEND SAUDI ARABIA...

TWO, LIBERATE KUWAIT! AND THREE, RESTORE PEACE AND STABILITY TO THE REGION. THAT'S WHAT I'VE BEEN ORDERED TO DO, AND THAT'S WHAT I'M DAMN WELL GOING TO DO! IS THAT CLEAR?

YES, SIR, IT...
YO, GENERAL! WHY DON'T YOU PART THE RED SEA WHILE YOU'RE AT IT?

YOU HAVE A QUESTION, SOLDIER?
YES, SIR. YOU SAY ONE OF OUR OBJECTIVES IS THE ESTABLISHMENT OF PEACE AND STABILITY IN THE REGION...

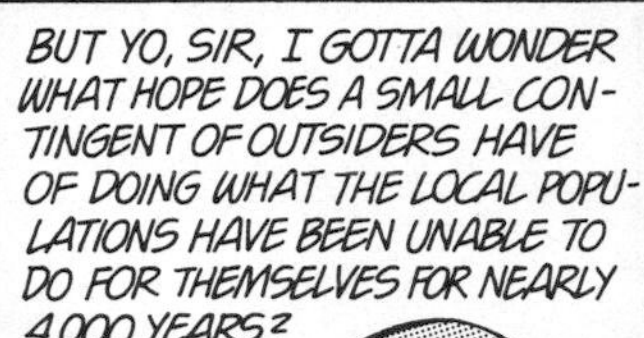
BUT YO, SIR, I GOTTA WONDER WHAT HOPE DOES A SMALL CONTINGENT OF OUTSIDERS HAVE OF DOING WHAT THE LOCAL POPULATIONS HAVE BEEN UNABLE TO DO FOR THEMSELVES FOR NEARLY 4,000 YEARS?

SO. YOU'VE READ HISTORY, SON.
NOT REALLY, SIR. JUST THE IN-FLIGHT MAGAZINE.

SO WHEN'S BOOPSIE GETTING OVER HERE, MAN?
SHE'S NOT. SHE GOT CANCELED OUT...

COMMAND THINKS CONCERTS ARE A SECURITY RISK. THEY'RE ALSO WORRIED ABOUT OFFENDING THE SAUDIS. SO NO DANCING BABES FOR THANKSGIVING!

NOW, THAT'S A DAMN SHAME...
YOU SAID IT. I WONDER WHO WE'LL GET INSTEAD.

HOLD IT! SHOULDN'T I BE WEARING CAMOUFLAGE FATIGUES?
UM... I THINK YOU'LL BE OKAY, SIR.

ATTENTION, CAMPERS! WE'VE GOT **COMPANY**!
N.Y. 10,534
LOS ANGELES
BOSTON

YES, AT 1400 HOURS—THAT'S 2:00 P.M. FOR YOU RESERVISTS—THIS BASE CAMP SOMEWHERE IN THE MID-EAST WILL BE PRIVILEGED TO HOST THE **C-IN-C HISSELF!**

SO IF YOU SERVICE GUYS 'N' GALS WILL JUST SHOW UP IN DRESS FORMATION IN FULL GEAR, THE PREZ HAS PROMISED TO DELIVER A FEW BOMBSHELLS... OOPS, I MEAN, CHOICE WORDS! HA, HA!

HE'S GONNA **KILL** US... OOPS! I MEAN, PUT US AWAY... NO...
DO WE HAVE FUN HERE OR WHAT?
SURE IS RAINING TURKEYS THIS WEEK.

THINK THE BUSHMAN'S GONNA TELL US WHY WE'RE HERE?
HE ALREADY HAS. DIDN'T YOU GET YOUR WALLET CARD?

WHAT WAL-LET CARD?
"WHY WE ARE HERE." IT LISTS BUSH'S KEY POSITIONS. THEY MADE UP 250,000 COPIES.

THEY PRINTED 250,000 COPIES OF GEORGE BUSH'S **POSITIONS** ON SOMETHING?
UH... YEAH. WHY NOT?

OKAY, I STILL BELIEVE IN THE FIRST ONE, BUT THE SECOND AND THIRD ARE ON THE TABLE...
VERY GOOD, SIR.

HEY, I COULDN'T BE HAPPIER TO BE WITH YOU BRAVE MEN AND GALS TODAY. I'M SERI-OUS ABOUT THAT.

I KNOW A LOT OF YOU WOULD RATHER BE HOME WITH YOUR LOVED ONES RIGHT NOW. SO, LET'S REVIEW THESE GOOD, GOOD REASONS WHY WE'RE HERE IN THE GULF...

IF EVERYONE COULD WHIP OUT THEIR "WHY WE ARE HERE" WAL-LET CARDS AND READ SILENTLY WHILE I READ ALOUD...

"IF HISTORY TEACHES US ANY-THING..."
"IF HIS-TORY TEACHES US ANY-THING..."
"RENT TWO VIDEOS, GET ONE FREE..."

THIS IS ROLAND HEDLEY WITH THE PRESIDENT, BUT I CAN'T SAY WHERE, JUST IN CASE THERE ARE ANY TERRORISTS TUNED IN...

TODAY PRESIDENT BUSH CONTINUES TO ENTERTAIN THE TROOPS HE DIS-PATCHED TO THIS REGION — AND IT'S BEEN **SOME** SHOW!

SURE, THERE ARE PROFESSIONAL COMICS LIKE JAY LENO OVER HERE THIS HOLIDAY, BUT IT'S PRESIDENT BUSH WHO'S BEEN PUTTING THE MEN AWAY!

OH, BY THE WAY — I'M **TOTALLY** OPPOSED TO TAXES AGAIN!
HA! HA! HA! HA!!
STOP IT! **STOP** IT!